ISLAM ACCORDING TO MUHAMMAD

ISLAM ACCORDING TO MUHAMMAD

NOT YOUR NEIGHBOR

Stephen M. Kirby Ph.D.

ISBN-10: 1499691688

ISBN-13: 978-1499691689

CreateSpace
Charleston, South Carolina

For Abdul Ameer

and all those like him who are striving to ensure that Islam is correctly understood.

The Canon of Islam

Islam does not, like Christianity, have a clergy. There is no temporal or even spiritual institute that holds it together or unifies it. So how has it held together—and indeed, flourished—for the last fourteen centuries approximately, when its scholars and temporal policymakers keep changing and dying out over time? How has it remained so homogeneous that the Islam of 1900 CE was doctrinally exactly the same as the Islam of 700 CE? Where have its internal checks and balances come from?

The answer is that Islam has a traditional canon: a collection of sacred texts which everyone has agreed are authoritative and definitive, and which 'fix' the principles of belief, practice, law, theology and doctrine throughout the ages. All that Muslim scholars (called ulema and muftis or sheikhs and imams) have left to do is to interpret these texts and work out their practical applications and details (and the principles of interpretation and elaboration are themselves 'fixed' by these texts), so that in Islam a person is only considered learned to the extent that he can demonstrate his knowledge of these texts. This does not mean that Islam is a religion of limitations for these texts are a vast ocean and their principles can be inwardly worked out almost infinitely in practice. It does mean, however, that Islam is 'fixed' and has certain limits beyond which it will not go.

The Muslim 500 – The World's 500 Most Influential Muslims 2013/14, The Royal Islamic Strategic Studies Centre (Amman, Jordan), p. 21

Islamic Modernism

Islamic modernism is a reform movement started by politically-minded urbanites with scant knowledge of traditional Islam. These people had witnessed and studied Western technology and socio-political ideas, and realized that the Islamic world was being left behind technologically by the West and had become too weak to stand up to it. They blamed this weakness on what they saw as 'traditional Islam,' which they thought held them back and was not 'progressive' enough. They thus called for a complete overhaul of Islam, including—or rather in particular—Islamic law (sharia) and doctrine (aqida). Islamic modernism remains popularly an object of derision and ridicule, and is scorned by traditional Muslims and fundamentalists alike.

The Muslim 500 – The World's 500 Most Influential Muslims 2013/14, The Royal Islamic Strategic Studies Centre (Amman, Jordan), p. 29

Innovation is Heresy

Muhammad said: *The most truthful speech is Allah's Speech, and the best guidance is the guidance of Muhammad. The worst matters are the newly invented (in religion), every newly invented matter is an innovation, and every innovation is a heresy, and every heresy is in the Fire.*

   Tafsir Ibn Kathir, Vol. 2, p. 588

Muhammad bin Jarir reported that Ibn 'Abbas said that the Prophet said, 'Whoever explains the Qur'an with his opinion or with what he has no knowledge of, then let him assume his seat in the Fire.'

   Tafsir Ibn Kathir, Vol. 1, pp. 32-33

Table of Contents

Introduction

Just because an individual Muslim does not, at the moment, want to adhere to the commands of Allah in the Koran and the teachings of Muhammad, doesn't mean those commands and teachings are no longer valid. They are still valid, timeless Islamic doctrine, to which that Muslim can return at any time.

The only way to understand Islam is to join with the vast majority of the world's Muslims and learn it as Muhammad taught it. He used two, interwoven approaches to instruct his Muslim followers. The first consisted of proclaiming the perfect, unchangeable, timeless commands of Allah, "revealed" to Muhammad and later codified in one book, the Koran. The second consisted of using his own examples and teachings (*the Sunnah*) to provide an understanding of the verses in the Koran and to address matters not covered in those verses. The significance of the *Sunnah* stemmed from the fact that Muhammad spoke for Allah (4:80), the Koran specifically commanded Muslims to obey Muhammad (59:7), and the Koran stated that Muhammad was the timeless standard by which Muslims should conduct themselves if they hoped to meet Allah (33:21).

The Koran and the *Sunnah* are the sources for most of the Islamic doctrine. And the Koran said that Muslims are not allowed to disagree once Allah and Muhammad have *decreed* a matter:

Chapter 33, Verse 36

It is not for a believer, man or woman, when Allah and His Messenger, have decreed a matter that they should have any option in their decision. And whoever disobeys Allah and His Messenger, he had indeed strayed into a plain error.

In addition, Allah stated that the religion of Islam was perfected and finalized during the time of Muhammad:

Chapter 5, Verse 3

> ...This day, I have perfected your religion for you, completed My Favour upon you, and have chosen for you Islam as your religion...

So if it is stated in the Koran and/or the *Sunnah*, a Muslim is not allowed to disagree. This underscores the significance of the Koran and the *Sunnah* in understanding Islam. And Islam was *perfected* during the time of Muhammad, so religious innovation is heresy.

But what about the miscellaneous issues not covered by these two sources, and that seem to hover around the edges of Islam and crop up from time-to-time? For these, Muslims look for a consensus opinion of authoritative Islamic scholars.

In spite of the fact that the majority of the doctrines of Islam were established in the 7th Century and are as valid today as they were then, there seems to be an increasing confusion about what Islam teaches and what it means to be a Muslim. This stems largely from a reluctance, and sometimes even a fear, to examine those doctrines by giving Islam the same scrutiny that has been given to other religions.

There seems to be more of a preference for a neighborly, comforting version of Islam that can be found among those who appear to know very little about the religion, and/or believe they can ignore the Koran and Muhammad and use their own personal perspectives to explain the "true" doctrines of Islam. As part of this neighborly approach, adjectives such as "radical" and "moderate" have become almost mandatory when discussing Islam; and the term "radical" seems to be most commonly used when discussing violence claimed to have been done in the name of Islam.

The purpose of my research and writing is to assist in clearing up this confusion by focusing on the Islam taught by Muhammad. In doing so, I have taken to heart Muhammad's prohibitions against introducing innovations to Islam, or using my personal opinion to interpret the verses of the Koran and his teachings; when opinions and interpretations are called for, I rely on authoritative Islamic scholars. As a by-product of this approach, I am also striving to clear up myths about Islam, whether perpetuated by Muslims or non-Muslims, and I let the chips fall where they may.

The focus of my last book, *Letting Islam Be Islam: Separating Truth From Myth*,[1] was on introducing the reader to concepts and sources of

---

[1]   In the Fall of 2013 this book was reviewed in *Islamic Literature*, Issue No. 73, 2013. This is a university magazine published online by the Sharia Branch of Islamic Studies, Beirut Islamic University, Beirut, Lebanon.

Letting Islam Be Islam: Separating Truth From Myth

The book, written by Dr. Stephen Kirby, is based on the authentic, historical Islamic sources and the writings of new researchers as well as the foundation of Islamic thinking today. Through it all, the book provides a very deep understanding of the Koran and the Sunnah in an effort to help the Muslim and the non-Muslim know and understand current Muslim behavior. The book provides help understanding the basic relationship of Muslims with each other and with non-Muslims. It consists of 19 chapters which include: interpretations, hadith, sirah (Mohammad's biography), the concept of abrogation, the prophet hood of Mohammad, peace be on Him, the Islamic religion and all the monotheistic religions, sharia, women, slavery, apostasy, interfaith regulations according to Omar, the five daily prayers, heaven, and American Muslims.

The book is an excellent resource to guide you in understanding the enormous plethora of information about Islam. Whatever the motivation of those writings, whether it is out of knowledge, intelligence, fear, ignorance, deceit, or truce, you will understand them better after reading this book.

[Information and translation provided by Dr. Mark Christian]

information fundamental to understanding Islam. These concepts and that information are found in the Koran, the *Sunnah*, and the writings and consensus of authoritative Islamic scholars. I then applied them to help the reader gain an understanding of topics that included, *inter alia*, the treatment of women, teachings about Jews and Christians, the significance of the final chapter of the Koran, and the prospects for any fundamental change to Islam.

The focus of this book is on applying those concepts and that information to more current events. For instance, does Islamic doctrine support atrocities committed against non-combatants by *jihadists*? Can Islamic doctrine provide the basis for mothers lauding the deaths of their sons in "suicide" missions? As I show in this book, the answer to both is *yes*.

I also look at the doctrinal bases for the modern efforts to redefine *Jihad* so that the word simply means a personal struggle to improve oneself, instead of fighting non-Muslims in the Cause of Allah. As I show, the doctrinal bases for this attempted redefinition are, at best, weak.

The claim that the Muslim country of Morocco was the first country to recognize the new United States is frequently heard from, and emphatically made by, many Muslim-Americans. Although addressing

---

International Institute of Islamic Thought – Book Review (14)
(http://eiiit.org/resources/eiiit/eiiit_article_read.asp?articleID=1023)

Letting Islam Be Islam: Separating Truth From Myth, Dr. Stephen M. Kirby, CreateSpace Independent Publishing Platform (October 2, 2012), 402 pages

عنوان الكتاب بالعربية: "ليكون الإسلام هو الإسلام: فصل الحقيقة عن الخرافة". اعتمد مؤلف الكتاب الدكتور (ستيفين كيربي) على المصادر الإسلامية التاريخية الأصيلة، وكتابات الباحثين الجدد، إضافة إلى أسس التفكير الإسلامي اليوم. ومن خلال ذلك كله، يقدم الكتاب فهماً أعمق للقرآن والسُّنة بحيث يساعد المسلم وغير المسلم على معرفة السلوكيات الراهنة وفهمها، وعلى فهم أسس علاقة المسلمين ببعضهم بعضاً وبغير المسلمين. يتكون الكتاب من تسعة عشر فصلاً: شملت علوم التفسير والحديث والسيرة، ومبدأ النسخ، ونبوة محمد عليه الصلاة والسلام، ودين السلام، والأديان التوحيدية، والشريعة والمرأة، وقضية الرق، والردة، والعهدة العمرية، والصلوات الخمس، والجنة، والمسلمون الأميركيون. الكتاب دليل ممتاز لتوجيه الفهم للتدفق الهائل للإسهاب في الحديث عن الإسلام، سواء أكان ذلك عن علم أم ذكاء أم خوف أم تهدئة أم جهل أم خداع.

iv

that topic does not fit in with the theme of this book, it is important to show the error of this claim. For that reason, I have addressed this topic in *Appendix 5*. The correct answer: France.

To clarify, verses in the Koran are mentioned two ways in this book: Chapter 9, Verse 5, or 9:5.

The majority of the sources used in this book are English translations of authoritative Islamic works, translated by Muslims and published by Muslim publishing houses. In many of the *hadiths* and verses of the Koran that I quote in this book you will see words in parentheses. These words have been inserted by the particular translator to assist the reader in better understanding the translation.

As with my other books, I have generally erred on the side of quoting at length, instead of providing a summary. This allows, for example, a statement by Muhammad to be seen in its full context, and minimizes a claim commonly heard when talking about Islam: *That quote was taken out of context*.

All dates used in this book are Anno Domini.

> *How can you use the term radical without first identifying the norm? Normative Islam is based on the unabrogated commands of Allah in the Koran, and the examples and teachings of Muhammad (the Sunnah). If the Koran and the Sunnah support a Muslim's actions, that Muslim is not radical, he is devout.*

Stephen M. Kirby
July 7, 2014

v

A Return to Islam

For many years now, especially since the terrorist attacks of September 11th, we have heard that Islam is a Religion of Peace, and that the "suicide bombers" and *jihadists* have "hijacked" that religion and are not following its true teachings. When discussing Islam, adjectives such as "radical," "extremist," and "moderate" seem obligatory. And these discussions usually end by concluding that the "moderate" Muslims are the true followers of Islam.

Yet we frequently see acts of terrorism and other violence that are claimed to have been done in the name of Islam. This creates a disconnect between what we hear and what we see. And this disconnect stems from the fact that we have strayed too far away from Islam in our discussions. It is time to turn away from the personal, religious interpretations of individual Muslims. It is time to return to Islam. Here is why.

For years we have been told that Islam is a religion of peace. Yet on September 11, 2001, Muslim terrorists hijacked four airplanes and used them to kill almost 3,000 people on American soil; Osama Bin Laden later said that these Muslims died as martyrs because they were acting in the name of Islam and fighting for the Cause of Allah.

Too often we read about "suicide bombers" who strap on explosives, or load their vehicles with explosives, and then blow themselves up to kill and injure those around them; the videos left by some of these bombers point out that these missions were done in the name of Islam.

We are told that Islam is a tolerant religion that does not force itself on non-Muslims and is respectful of Judaism and Christianity. However there are regular reports coming out of countries in the Middle East and Africa about Muslim persecution and murder of Jews and Christians, and forced conversions of Christians to Islam.

We are told that Islam is a tolerant religion, yet cartoons about Muhammad in a Danish newspaper in 2005 caused destruction and death in parts of the Middle East because there were Muslims who said that these cartoons denigrated the prophet Muhammad and ridiculed Islam; and there have been repeated attempts by Muslims on the life of Kurt Westergaard, the cartoonist responsible for those drawings.

In 2011, a French weekly satirical newspaper named *Charlie Hebdo* ran an edition with a cover page showing a cartoon of Muhammad and that the newspaper's name had been changed to *Charia Hebdo*. There were international protests and the office of the newspaper was firebombed. Nevertheless, in September 2012 the newspaper again published satirical cartoons of Muhammad. Police went on alert in Paris and guarded the newspaper's office. The French government ordered the closure of French embassies, schools and cultural centers in 20 Muslim countries on the next Friday, the Muslim day of prayer.

In these two instances involving the Danish and French newspapers, most of the American press declined to re-print the cartoons or the satirical covers. The Associated Press would not distribute them. Much of the American press rationalized their silence as simply showing respect for a great religion, a religion of peace.

There is a disconnect between what we in the United States regularly hear about Islam and what we see being done in the name of Islam. Why?

Because according to the current paradigm, acts of violence done in the name of Islam are done by *jihadists*, *Islamists*, or *radical Muslims*. These are labels used in an effort to differentiate these violent acts from the religion of Islam. According to this paradigm, the *Islamists* are the ones who have supposedly "hijacked" the "Religion of Peace," and picked and chosen among the doctrines of Islam, ignoring Islam's supposed inherently peaceful, tolerant teachings.

The contrast is to be found in the "Moderate Muslims," who peacefully practice what is considered "true" Islam in open-minded, tolerant coexistence with other religions, and, although not widely vocal about it, supposedly do not support the *Islamists*. According to this paradigm, the Moderate Muslims are the true Muslims.

However, there are some important considerations. For example, the *Islamists* believe in cutting off the hands of thieves; the Moderate Muslims don't. But 5:38 of the Koran commands this punishment for thieves:[1]

> *And (as for) the male thief and the female thief, cut off (from the wrist joint) their (right) hands as a recompense for that which they committed, a punishment by way of example from Allah. And Allah is All-Powerful, All-Wise.*

And Muhammad referred to this as "one of the legal punishments prescribed by Allah,"[2] and ordered the hands of many thieves to be cut off.

The *Islamists* believe in stoning adulterers; the Moderate Muslims don't. The Koran does not mention stoning as the punishment for adultery. However, Muhammad said that he was "the first to revive the order of God and His book and to practice it [stoning for adulterers],"[3] and he commanded many an adulterer to be stoned to death.[4]

---

[1] Unless otherwise indicated, the verses of the Koran used in this book are from *The Noble Qur'an*, trans. Muhammad Muhsin Khan and Muhammad Taqi-ud-Din Al-Hilali (Riyadh, Kingdom of Saudi Arabia: Darussalam, 2007).

[2] Muhammad bin Ismail bin Al-Mughirah Al-Bukhari, *Sahih Al-Bukhari*, trans. Muhammad Muhsin Khan, Vol. 5 (Riyadh, Kingdom of Saudi Arabia: Darussalam, 1997), Book 64, No. 4304, pp. 361-362. This story was also reported by Aisha - see *Sahih Al-Bukhari*, Vol. 4, Book 60, No. 3475, p. 427; and Abu Dawud Sulaiman bin Al-Ash'ath bin Ishaq, *Sunan Abu Dawud*, trans. Yaser Qadhi, Vol. 5 (Riyadh, Kingdom of Saudi Arabia: Darussalam, 2008), No. 4373, pp. 27-28.

[3] Muhammad ibn Ishaq, *The Life of Muhammad (Sirat Rasul Allah)*, trans. Alfred Guillaume (Karachi: Oxford University Press, 2007), p. 267. A similar statement by Muhammad was reported in Abu'l Hussain 'Asakir-ud-Din Muslim

3

The *Islamists* believe that an apostate from Islam should be killed, preferably by beheading; Moderate Muslims don't. The Koran states that apostates can be killed:

Chapter 4, Verse 89

> ...*But if they turn back (from Islam), take (hold of) them and kill them wherever you find them...*

On many occasions Muhammad said that those who left Islam should be killed,[5] and he even specifically said

> *If someone changes his religion – then strike off his head!*[6]

The *Islamists* believe that *Jihad* means fighting in a holy war against the non-Muslims; Moderate Muslims say *Jihad* is a personal effort to make

---

bin Hajjaj al-Qushayri al-Naisaburi, *Sahih Muslim*, trans. Abdul Hamid Siddiqi, Vol. 5 (New Delhi: Adam Publishers and Distributors, 2008), No. 1700, p. 140; Muhammad bin Yazeed ibn Majah Al-Qazwini, *Sunan Ibn Majah*, trans. Nasiruddin al-Khattab, Vol. 3 (Riyadh, Kingdom of Saudi Arabia: Darussalam, 2007), No. 2558, pp. 466-467; and *Sunan Abu Dawud*, Vol. 5, Nos. 4447-4448, pp. 69-71.

[4]   A college professor who is a Muslim acknowledged to me that Muhammad had ordered the stoning of adulterers, but he rationalized it by stating that Muhammad had only ordered this punishment if the person had actually confessed to the adultery. So a personal confession by an adulterer justifies this brutal form of execution.

[5]   E.g., *Sahih Al-Bukhari*, Vol. 4, Book 56, No. 3017, p. 159; Vol. 9, Book 87, No. 6878, p. 20; Vol. 9, Book 87, No. 6899, pp. 31-32; Vol. 9, Book 88, No. 6923, pp. 46-47; and Vol. 9, Book 93, No. 7157, pp. 168-169; and *Sahih Muslim*, Vol. 5, No. 1676, pp. 118-119; and Vol. 6, No. 1733R3, pp. 240-241.

[6]   Malik ibn Anas ibn Malik ibn Abi 'Amir al-Asbahi, *Al-Muwatta of Imam Malik ibn Anas: The First Formulation of Islamic Law*, trans. Aisha Abdurrahman Bewley (Inverness, Scotland: Madinah Press, 2004), 36.18.15.

oneself a better person. But Muhammad repeatedly spoke about *Jihad* in the context of fighting against non-Muslims and said that any Muslim

> *who died but did not fight in the way of Allah nor did he*
> *express any desire (or determination) for Jihad died the*
> *death of a hypocrite.*[7]

And 9:111 of the Koran promises Paradise to those who die while fighting in the Cause of Allah:

> *Verily, Allah has purchased of the believers their lives and*
> *their properties for (the price) that theirs shall be*
> *Paradise. They fight in Allah's Cause, so they kill (others)*
> *and are killed. It is a promise in truth which is binding on*
> *Him in the Taurat (Torah) and the Injil (Gospel) and the*
> *Qur'an. And who is truer to his covenant than Allah?*
> *Then rejoice in the bargain which you have concluded.*
> *That is the supreme success.*

9:5 of the Koran is referred to as the *Verse of the Sword* by authoritative Islamic scholars. The *Islamists* follow its commands while the Moderate Muslims don't have a lot to say about it. This verse commands Muslims to besiege, ambush, fight and kill non-Muslims (*Mushrikun*) until the remaining non-Muslims "repent" and become Muslims:

> *Then when the Sacred Months (the 1st, 7th, 11th, and 12th*
> *months of the Islamic calendar) have passed, then kill the*

---

[7] *Sahih Muslim*, Vol. 6, No. 1910, p. 289. Muhammad also said that meeting Allah without any marks from *Jihad*/fighting indicated the Muslim had "a defect" or "a deficiency." See, respectively, Abu 'Eisa Mohammad ibn 'Eisa at-Tirmidhi, *Jami' At-Tirmidhi*, trans. Abu Khaliyl, Vol. 3 (Riyadh, Kingdom of Saudi Arabia: Darussalam, 2007), No. 1666, p. 412; and *Sunan Ibn Majah*, Vol. 4, No. 2763, p. 47.

For a detailed examination of the modern effort to redefine *Jihad* as a personal struggle to make oneself a better person, see Chapter 12, *Redefining Jihad.*

*Mushrikun wherever you find them, and capture them and
besiege them, and lie in wait for them in every ambush.
But if they repent [by rejecting Shirk (polytheism) and
accept Islamic Monotheism] and perform As-Salat (the
prayers), and give Zakat (obligatory charity), then leave
their way free. Verily, Allah is Oft-Forgiving, Most
Merciful.*

The *Islamists* follow the commands of 9:29 of the Koran. This verse
commands Muslims to fight against Jews and Christians until those Jews
and Christians feel subdued and pay the *Jizyah*. The *Jizyah* is a tax
imposed on non-Muslims living under "protection" of an Islamic
government. Here is that verse:

*Fight against those who believe not in Allah, nor in the
Last Day, nor forbid that which has been forbidden by
Allah and His Messenger (Muhammad), and those who
acknowledge not the religion of truth (i.e. Islam) among
the people of the Scripture (Jews and Christians), until
they pay the Jizyah with willing submission, and feel
themselves subdued.*

The Moderate Muslims don't have much to say about this.

The *Islamists* say that those who criticize or ridicule Muhammad should be
killed. The Moderate Muslims don't have much to say about this either.
But Muhammad did. He personally ordered the killing of a number of
people who had ridiculed him.

And on one occasion a Muslim fatally stabbed his pregnant female slave
because she was disparaging Muhammad;[8] on another occasion, a Muslim

---

[8]   *Sunan Abu Dawud*, Vol. 5, No. 4361, pp. 20-21. This narration was also
reported in Abu 'Abdur-Rahman Ahmad bin Shu'aib bin 'Ali bin Sinan bin Bahr
An-Nasa'i, *Sunan An-Nasa'i*, trans. Nasiruddin al-Khattab, Vol. 5 (Riyadh,
Kingdom of Saudi Arabia: Darussalam, 2007), No. 4075, pp. 66-67; in this *hadith*
Muhammad said, "I bear witness that her blood is permissible."

strangled a Jewish woman to death because she was also disparaging Muhammad.[9] When Muhammad found out about these, he said there was to be no penalty imposed on those two Muslims.

And 33:57 of the Koran states that Allah curses anyone who annoys Allah and His Messenger Muhammad:

> *Verily, those who annoy Allah and His Messenger, Allah has cursed them in this world and in the Hereafter, and has prepared for them a humiliating torment.*

And one could annoy Muhammad by doing such things as claiming that he had faults or that he was not the Messenger of Allah. As Ibn Kathir, an authoritative Muslim scholar explained, to annoy Muhammad is to annoy Allah.[10]

Muslims consider the Koran to be the unchangeable, infallible, and eternal word of Allah. They believe that Muhammad spoke for Allah, and that he must be obeyed and his example followed. So we need to ask ourselves: Who are the true Muslims?

The reality is that the so-called *Islamists* are the true Muslims because they are following the commands of Allah found in the Koran, and the teachings and example of Muhammad. It is the so-called Moderate Muslims who are picking and choosing among those doctrines and teachings. And this salad bar approach to Islam is condemned by the Koran and by Muhammad. The Koran states that the religion of Islam was perfected and finalized during the time of Muhammad:

---

[9]   *Sunan Abu Dawud*, Vol. 5, No. 4362, p. 21.

[10]   Abu Al-Fida' 'Imad Ad-Din Isma'il bin 'Umar bin Kathir Al-Qurashi Al-Busrawi, *Tafsir Ibn Kathir* (Abridged), trans. Jalal Abualrub, et al., Vol. 8 (Riyadh, Kingdom of Saudi Arabia: Darussalam, 2000), pp. 42-43.

Chapter 5, Verse 3

> ...*This day, I have perfected your religion for you, completed My Favour upon you, and have chosen for you Islam as your religion...*

The Koran cannot be changed:

Chapter 15, Verse 9

> *Verily, We, it is We Who have sent down the Dhikr (i.e. the Qur'an) and surely We will guard it (from corruption).*

The Koran prohibits picking and choosing among its verses:

Chapter 2, Verse 85

> ...*Then do you believe in a part of the Scripture and reject the rest? Then what is the recompense of those who do so among you, except disgrace in the life of this world, and on the Day of Resurrection they shall be consigned to the most grievous torment. And Allah is not unaware of what you do.*

Muhammad said:

> *It was narrated from Ibn 'Abbas that the Messenger of Allah said: "Whoever denies a Verse of the Qur'an, it is permissible to strike his neck (i.e. execute him)..."*[11]

---

[11]   *Sunan Ibn Majah*, Vol. 3, No. 2539, p. 455.

Muhammad also took a dim view of the idea of making changes to Islam. He said:

> *The most truthful speech is Allah's Speech, and the best guidance is the guidance of Muhammad. The worst matters are the newly invented (in religion), every newly invented matter is an innovation, and every innovation is a heresy, and every heresy is in the Fire.*[12]

And Muhammad said that Allah "cursed him who accommodated an innovator (in religion)."[13]

Muhammad even said it was legal to kill a Muslim who introduced innovations and new ideas into Islam:

> *Narrated 'Abdullah: Allah's Messenger said, "The blood of a Muslim who confesses that La ilaha illallah (none has the right to be worshipped but Allah) and that I am the Messenger of Allah, cannot be shed except in three cases:...(3) the one who turns renegade from Islam (apostate) and leaves the group of Muslims (by innovating heresy, new ideas and new things, etc. in the Islamic religion)."*[14]

And Muhammad talked about being in Paradise to greet the Muslims who died after him, and seeing some of those Muslims taken away because of changes they had made to Islam after he died:

> *...There will come to me some people whom I know and they know me, and then a barrier will be set up between me and them." Abu Sa'id Al-Khudri added that the*

---

[12]   *Tafsir Ibn Kathir*, Vol. 2, p. 588.

[13]   *Sahih Muslim*, Vol. 6, No. 1978R2, p. 329.

[14]   *Sahih Al-Bukhari*, Vol. 9, Book 87, No. 6878, p. 20.

*Prophet further said, "I will say those people are from me
(i.e. they are my followers). It will be said, 'You do not
know what new changes and new things (heresies) they
did after you.' Then I will say, 'Far removed (from
mercy), far removed (from mercy), those who changed,
did new things in (the religion) after me!'".*[15]

And once an issue has been decided in the Koran and/or in the teachings of
Muhammad, it is blasphemy for a Muslim to disagree with that decision.
This is plainly stated a number of times in the Koran, e.g.:

Chapter 33, Verse 36

> *It is not for a believer, man or woman, when Allah and
> His Messenger, have decreed a matter that they should
> have any option in their decision. And whoever disobeys
> Allah and His Messenger, he has indeed strayed into a
> plain error.*

Chapter 59, Verse 7

> *...And whatsoever the Messenger (Muhammad) gives you,
> take it; and whatsoever he forbids you, abstain (from it).
> And fear Allah; verily, Allah is Severe in punishment.*

Chapter 4, Verse 115

> *And whoever contradicts and opposes the Messenger
> (Muhammad) after the right path has been shown clearly
> to him, and follows other than the believers' way, We shall
> keep him in the path he has chosen, and burn him in Hell -
> what an evil destination!*

---

[15] *Sahih Al-Bukhari*, Vol. 9, Book 92, Nos. 7050-7051, pp. 123-124.

It is time to repair the disconnect between what we see and what we hear about Islam. It is time to stop uncritically believing the personal perspectives on Islam of individual Muslims who happen to be our neighbors or with whom we work. The reality is that if the personal opinion of your Muslim neighbor or co-worker goes against what Muhammad taught, or what the Koran commands, or the consensus of authoritative Islamic scholars, then that personal opinion carries no weight within the greater Muslim community - the *Ummah*. Because the Islam believed in by the vast majority of the *Ummah* is the Islam "revealed" to and taught by Muhammad, not that of your neighbor or co-worker.

It is time to turn our focus and understanding to the one true Islam, the Islam as taught by Muhammad, commanded by the verses of the Koran, and agreed to by authoritative Islamic scholars. It is time to understand that your Muslim neighbor or co-worker might not adhere to it at the moment, but anytime Muslims want to, they can return to that one true Islam.

The Boston Marathon Bombers' Mom and *Umm Nidal*

On April 23, 2013, Zubeidat Tsarnaeva, the mother of Boston Marathon bombers Tamerlan and Dzhokhar Tsarnaev, was interviewed by CNN and made statements that had many people scratching their heads. The video of this interview can be found at many places on the internet.[16] Here were her comments:

> *If they are going to kill him* [Dzhokhar], *I don't care. My, my oldest one* [Tamerlan] *has been killed and I don't care. I don't care if my youngest one is going to be killed today. So I want the world to hear this. And, I don't care if I am going to get killed too. OK? And I will say Allahu Akbar.*

This resulted in many commentators asking how a mother can say such things. Of course these commentators knew little, if anything about Islam.

Here is an explanation for why she said it:

1. The only guaranteed way for a Muslim to get into Paradise is to die as a *jihadist*, a martyr fighting in the cause of Allah. This is a promise to Muslims made in Chapter 9, Verse 111 of the Koran:

---

[16]   E.g., http://www.thegatewaypundit.com/2013/04/whoa-zubeidat-tsarnaeva-tells-cnn-i-dont-care-if-my-youngest-son-is-killed-i-dont-care-if-i-am-killed-i-will-say-allahu-akbar-video/.

*Verily, Allah has purchased of the believers their
lives and their properties for (the price) that theirs
shall be Paradise. They fight in Allah's Cause, so
they kill (others) and are killed. It is a promise in
truth which is binding on Him in the Taurat (Torah)
and the Injil (Gospel) and the Qur'an. And who is
truer to his covenant than Allah? Then rejoice in the
bargain which you have concluded. That is the
supreme success.*

For anybody else, it is left entirely up to Allah, and there are no
guarantees, regardless of how one lived, because Allah is all
powerful; otherwise, guarantees would restrict Allah's power.

2. Muhammad was asked what "fighting in the cause of Allah" meant.
   He replied,

   *"He who fights that Allah's Word (i.e. Allah's
   Religion of Islamic Monotheism) should be superior,
   fights in Allah's Cause."*[17]

3. Dzhokhar Tsarnaev told investigators that he and his brother were
   motived by a desire to fight for Islam; they were fighting in Allah's
   cause and therefore guaranteed Paradise if they died.

4. Once in Paradise, each of them would get 72 virgin wives and be able
   to intercede with Allah for 70 of their relatives. Here is the *hadith*
   that explains it:

   *Al-Miqdam bin Ma'diykarib narrated that the
   Messenger of Allah said: "There are six things with
   Allah for the martyr: He is forgiven with the first
   flow of blood (he suffers), he is shown his place in
   Paradise, he is protected from punishment in the*

---

[17]   *Sahih Al-Bukhari*, Vol. 1, Book 3, No. 123, p. 128.

grave, secured from the greatest terror, the crown of dignity is placed upon his head - and its gems are better than the world and what is in it - he is married to seventy-two wives among Al-Huril-'Ayn of Paradise, and he may intercede for seventy of his close relatives."[18]

5. Zubeidat ended her comments with the phrase *Allahu Akbar*. This phrase means *Allah is Greatest*, and shows that her comments were meant in a religious context.

So Zubeidat Tsarnaeva was simply lauding the fact that one or both of her sons would be in Paradise, and each would be able to make sure that other family members would join them. She was probably assuming she would be one of those family members.

Such an attitude on the part of a mother is not limited to Zubeidat Tsarnaeva. On March 17, 2013, a Palestinian woman named Mariam Farhat died. Even though she had never been in the military, she received a military funeral attended by 4,000 Palestinians. Why did she receive a military funeral? Because she had earned the nickname of *Umm Nidal* (Mother of the Struggle).[19]

---

[18]   *Jami' At-Tirmidhi*, Vol. 3, No. 1663, p. 410. The *Al-Huril-'Ayn* (*Houris, Hur*) are the very fair female virgins of Paradise.

[19]   The information about *Umm Nidal* was obtained from the following on-line articles, accessed on April 14, 2014:

1. "An Interview with the Mother of a Suicide Bomber," *Islam Review*, June 5, 2002, at http://www.islamreview.com/articles/interview.shtml.

2. Joel Greenberg, "Gaza explosion kills 6 Hamas militants," *Chicago Tribune*, February 17, 2003, at http://articles.chicagotribune.com/2003-02-17/news/0302170148_1_hamas-militants-gaza-city-gaza-strip.

3. "Suicide Bombers' Mother Elected to Palestinian Parliament," *ABC News*, January 26, 2006, at http://abcnews.go.com/WNT/story?id=1536576.

Umm Nidal first came to public attention in March 2002, when she appeared in a martyrdom video with her 17 year old son Muhammad:

> *In it, she was shown sending her son Muhammad to launch an attack against a Jewish settlement in Gush Katif, in the Gaza Strip. Knowing that the chances of him returning alive were slim, she kissed him and encouraged him to sacrifice his life. There is not the slightest hint of sadness in her face. All we can see is the smile of a woman imbued with the terrifying belief that death is a small price to pay on the path to achieving the ultimate goal. Armed with a rifle, grenades and the knowledge that he was fulfilling his mother's mission, Muhammad infiltrated the settlement of Atzmona and killed five young students attending the military preparatory academy there before he was gunned down by the IDF.*[20]

In this video, *Umm Nidal* had said

> *I wish I had 100 boys like Muhammad. I'd sacrifice them for the sake of God.*[21]

4. Elior Levy, "'Mother of martyrs' dies,'" *Ynetnews.com*, March 17, 2013, at http://www.ynetnews.com/articles/0,7340,L-4357578,00.html.

5. Shlomi Eldar, "'The Mother of Martyrs' Leaves Bloody Legacy," *Al Monitor*, March 19, 2013, at http://www.al-monitor.com/pulse/originals/2013/03/the-bloody-legacy-of-the-mother-of-martyrs.html#.

6. William Yardley, "Mariam Farhat, Known as 'Mother of Martyrs,' Dies at 64," *The New York Times*, March 20, 2013, at http://www.nytimes.com/2013/03/20/world/middleeast/mariam-farhat-palestinian-mother-of-martyrs-dies-at-64.html?_r=0.

[20] "'The Mother of Martyrs' Leaves Bloody Legacy."

[21] "'Mother of martyrs' dies.'"

On June 5, 2002, the London-based Arabic-language daily *Al-Sharq Al-Awsat* published an interview with *Umm Nidal*. When asked how Muhammad had come up with the idea of the "martyrdom" operation, she replied:

> *Jihad is a [religious] commandment imposed upon us. We must instill this idea in our sons' souls, all the time...What we see every day – massacres, destruction, bombing [of] homes – strengthened, in the souls of my sons, especially Muhammad, the love of Jihad and martyrdom.*[22]

When asked if she had had a role in instilling this idea in Muhammad, she replied

> *Allah be praised, I am a Muslim and I believe in Jihad. Jihad is one of the elements of the faith and this is what encouraged me to sacrifice Muhammad in Jihad for the sake of Allah. My son was not destroyed, he is not dead; he is living a happier life than I. Had my thoughts been limited to this world, I would not sacrifice Muhammad... Because I love my son, I encouraged him to die a martyr's death for the sake of Allah... Jihad is a religious obligation incumbent upon us, and we must carry it out. I sacrificed Muhammad as part of my obligation. This is an easy thing. There is no disagreement [among scholars] on such matters. The happiness in this world is an incomplete happiness; eternal happiness is life in the world to come, through martyrdom. Allah be praised, my son has attained this happiness.*[23]

In February 2003, *Umm Nidal's* second son, Nidal, was killed. It happened when Nidal and five other members of the military branch of Hamas were getting ready to assemble a booby-trapped glider for use in attacks on Israeli targets. They had removed it from the trunk of a car when it exploded, killing all six. It was believed that the glider was

---

[22]   "An Interview with the Mother of a Suicide Bomber."

[23]   Ibid.

detonated by a signal from an Israeli drone overhead. Nidal left behind a four year old son named Imad:

> *Ms. Farhat told The New York Times in 2004 that she had assured Imad that he would be reunited with his father. "You will be a martyr one day," Ms. Farhat said she had told Imad, "and then you will go and see your dad."[24]*

Umm Nidal lost her third son, Ruwad, in 2005. Ruwad had been specifically targeted by an Israel aerial strike. At Ruwad's funeral, *Umm Nidal* said,

> *I have four sons left…I hope that they all become martyrs.[25]*

She later told the Associated Press that although she cried for these dead sons,
> *jihad (holy war) comes ahead of everything, including my feelings as a mother.[26]*

And in a 2009 interview with *National Geographic Television*, she said this about her sons:

> *I brought them up to be martyrs. To become martyrs for the name of Allah.[27]*

Only by understanding the Islam of Muhammad can we understand the bases for the statements of these two mothers.

---

[24]   "Mariam Farhat, Known as 'Mother of Martyrs,' Dies at 64."

[25]   "'The Mother of Martyrs' Leaves Bloody Legacy."

[26]   "'Mother of martyrs' dies.'"

[27]   "Mariam Farhat, Known as 'Mother of Martyrs,' Dies at 64."

The Westgate Mall in Nairobi, Kenya

*The Westgate attack was a long-awaited glad tiding to the Believers
and a well deserved blow in the face of the disbelievers.*

Gaidi Mtaani, p. 3

The Westgate Mall was a modern, popular shopping attraction in Nairobi,
Kenya. September 21, 2013 was a pleasant Saturday afternoon, and on
that day at least 1,000 people were inside the four-story complex,
including many children. But it was also on that day that the mall was
attacked by members of *Al-Shabaab*, a Muslim *jihadist* group
headquartered in Somalia. Here is how it was later described in the
November 2013 special edition of *Gaidi Mtaani* [*On Terrorism Street*], the
official on-line magazine of *Al-Shabaab*:

> *Saturday 21st September 2013 was a normal day in Kenya
> and around the world. It was a normal weekend for the
> infidels living in Kenya with families going for outings
> and shoppers crowding the various malls to buy the latest
> clothes, shoes etc. Westgate Mall, situated in Nairobi's
> Westlands area, was not different to other malls as
> members of the affluent class went about their shopping
> and normal weekend activities. The mall was buzzing with
> activity, with an estimated 3,000 people walking in and
> out not aware of the fate which was about to befall them.*
>
> *Suddenly, gunshots rang out into the air and explosions
> were heard inside the mall causing confusion everywhere
> with people running helter skelter for their lives. News
> spread like wildfire in the social media (which has become
> the trend) and everyone was asking the one question:*

*"What was that?" Different local news channels tried to
give an explanation, with Kenyan media outlets
shamelessly stating that there were reports of robbery
inside the mall. That was a first in the history of Kenya;
'armed thugs' hurling explosives generously to the
waiting Kuffar* [disbelievers] *who were at that time staring
at death in the eyes. Later on the local media had to admit
that it was an attack by the Mujahideen.*[28]

It was not until September 24th that Kenyan forces were able to take back
the mall. By that time, the attackers had wounded about 200 people and
killed over 60 others; many of those killed had been tortured and mutilated
before being killed, and there were stories of captives being beheaded and
women being raped. But those who had initially been able to identify
themselves as being Muslim were able to go free.

Shortly after the attack, Shaykh Mukhtar Abu Zubayr, the leader of *Al-
Shabaab*, said in a speech:

*On Saturday 21 September 2013, and which was just 10
days after the anniversary date of the blessed 911
operations, a battle which is among the epic battles in the
history of Islam began in Nairobi...*[29]

Abu Zubayr mentioned a shortened variation of the following *hadith* in his
speech:

---

[28]   *Gaidi Mtaani*, Issue 4, November 2013, pp. 12-13. The pdf copy of this
magazine is available at: http://azelin.files.wordpress.com/2013/11/gaidi-mtaani-
issue-4.pdf. Accessed on November 18, 2013.

[29]   *Transcript: Speech of HSM Leader, Shaykh Mukhtar Abu Zubayr,
regarding the #Westgate Operation*, September 26, 2013; accessed on October 1,
2013 at http://somalimidnimo.com/salafi/2013/09/transcript-speech-of-hsm-
leader-shaykh-mukhtar-abu-zubayr-regarding-the-westgate-operation/. HSM is
the acronym for *Harakat al-Shabaab al-Mujahideen* (Movement of the Warrior
Youth). See *Appendix 2* for the complete transcript.

It was narrated that 'Amr bin 'Abasah said: "I came to
the Prophet and said: 'O Messenger of Allah, which Jihad
is best'? He said: '(That of a man) whose blood is shed
and his horse is wounded.'"[30]

Among the verses from the Koran he quoted was Chapter 8, Verse 17:

You killed them not, but Allah killed them. And you
(Muhammad) threw not when you did throw, but Allah
threw, that He might test the believers by a fair trial from
Him. Verily, Allah is All-Hearer, All-Knower.

Abu Zubayr called those taking part in the attack *Mujahideen* (fighters for
the Cause of Allah). And he also called them *Mujahideen Martyrdom
Seekers.* Why? Here we can see again the importance of understanding
Islam.

As was pointed out previously, the only guaranteed way for Muslims to
get into Paradise is to die as *Mujahideen.* This is a promise to Muslims
that Allah made in Chapter 9, Verse 111 of the Koran:

Verily, Allah has purchased of the believers their
lives and their properties for (the price) that theirs
shall be Paradise. They fight in Allah's Cause, so
they kill (others) and are killed...

The fact that the *Al-Shabaab* attackers were considered *Mujahideen*
fighting for the Cause of Allah was reiterated in the November 2013
special edition of *Gaidi Mtaani.* In this special edition the *Al-Shabaab*
fighters at the Westgate Mall were called *the lions of Islam* and repeatedly
referred to as *Mujahideen* engaging in *Jihad*; it was noted that:

---

[30]   This *hadith* is found in *Sunan Ibn Majah*, Vol. 4, No. 2794, p. 65.

Fighting (in Allah's Path) is an honour and hitting the Kuffar where it hurts is what the Mujahideen most relish.[31]

And

The Mujahideen who carried out the Badru Nairobi operation are part of the Harakat Al-Shabaab Al-Mujahideen's Martyrdom brigade; these are brothers who have volunteered to enter into enemy ranks and cause havoc before being killed by the enemy.[32]

And included among the enemies were the Jews:

The aftermath of the unexpected and devastating attacks against the Jewish owned Westgate Shopping Mall elicited either much praises from the supporters and sympathizers of the Mujahideen or amplified hullabaloo and castigations against the Warriors who carried out the operation.[33]

But the mall was more than just Jewish-owned, it was "Jewish":

The Kenyan media consistently disparaged the Mujahideen who attacked the Jewish Westgate Mall as cowards.[34]

So the attack on the "Jewish" Westgate Mall was done in the name of Islam and the attackers were *Mujahideen* who claimed to be the

---

[31]   *Gaidi Mtaani*, p. 15.

[32]   Ibid., p. 21.

[33]   Ibid., p. 20.

[34]   Ibid., p. 23.

21

instruments of Allah; they were not only fighting in Allah's cause, but seeking death in order to be guaranteed entrance into Paradise. There is even video from inside the mall showing some *Mujahideen* taking a break from the killing in order to perform their prayers.[35]

Abubaker Shariff Ahmed (better known as Makaburi), then-imam of the Musa mosque in Mombasa, Kenya, had this to say about the attack on the mall:

> *As per the Koran, as per the religion of Islam, Westgate was 100 percent justified.*[36]

But does Islamic doctrine really support the killing, torturing, mutilation, and beheading of non-combatant civilians, and the raping of female captives? We'll examine that question in detail in the next eight chapters.

---

[35]   1) http://www.youtube.com/watch?v=uxGST7V02UA;

2) http://www.cnn.com/2013/10/17/world/africa/kenya-mall-attack-footage/;

3) http://www.nydailynews.com/news/world/kenya-mall-video-shows-terrorists-casually-gun-shoppers-article-1.1488402.

[36]   "Hardline Kenya cleric, the face of homegrown radical Islam," *Africatime.com*, March 11, 2014. Accessed on March 31, 2014 at

http://en.africatime.com/articles/hardline-kenya-cleric-face-homegrown-radical-islam.

It is interesting to note what Makaburi had to say about "radical Islam" in this same article:

> *"Radical Islam is a creation of people who do not believe in Islam. We don't have radical Islam, we don't have moderates, we don't have extremists. Islam is one religion following the Koran and the Sunnah," said Makaburi.*

Makaburi was shot to death in Mombasa on April 1, 2014.

4

Killing of Non-Combatant
Women and Children

You might be thinking to yourself about claims that Islam generally prohibits the killing of non-combatant women and children,[37] and that Muhammad had specifically prohibited such killings. There are two popular *hadiths* that are often used to support these claims:

> *It has been reported from Sulaiman b. Buraid through his father that when the Messenger of Allah (may peace be upon him) appointed anyone as leader of an army or detachment he would especially exhort him to fear Allah and to be good to the Muslims who were with him. He would say: Fight in the name of Allah and in the way of Allah. Fight against those who disbelieve in Allah. Make a holy war... do not kill the children.[38]*

And

> *Ibn 'Umar narrated that a woman was found killed in one of the expeditions of the Messenger of Allah, so the*

---

[37]   Unless otherwise noted, the status as *non-combatant* is to be understood when I mention women and/or children in this chapter.

[38]   *Sahih Muslim*, Vol. 5, No. 1731R1, pp. 162-163. Variations of this narration from Buraid(ah) were also reported in *Sunan Ibn Majah*, Vol. 4, No. 2858, pp. 98-99; *Sunan Abu Dawud*, Vol. 3, No. 2613, p. 264; and *Jami' At-Tirmidhi*, Vol. 3, No. 1408, p. 193; and No. 1617, p. 376. A similar *hadith*, from a different narrator, is found in *Al-Muwatta of Imam Malik ibn Anas*, 21.3.11.

*Messenger of Allah rebuked that, and he prohibited killing
women and children.[39]*

So according to the first *hadith*, whenever Muhammad appointed anyone
to lead a Muslim army or detachment, he would issue an order that
children were not to be killed. And the second *hadith* states that
Muhammad prohibited the killing of women and children.

However, when the military actions of the Muslims during the life of
Muhammad are examined chronologically, one finds that instead of it
being a general, all-encompassing command issued by Muhammad to
every Muslim military leader, and a part of Islamic doctrine, the
prohibition against the killing of women and children was a specific,
situational prohibition based on Muhammad's judgments and the demands
of battle at the time.

The following examination of Muslim military actions during the life of
Muhammad is based mainly on a review of the relevant biographical
writings of seven authoritative Islamic scholars and of an award-winning,
modern biography of Muhammad.[40] A chronological overview of this
information can be found in *Appendix 3: Killing According to Muhammad.*

---

[39]   *Jami' At-Tirmidhi*, Vol. 3, No. 1569, pp. 341-342.

[40]   The works consulted:

Muhammad ibn 'Abdul Wahhab At-Tamimi, *Abridged Biography of Prophet
Muhammad*, ed. 'Abdur-Rahman bin Nasir Al-Barrak, 'Abdul 'Azeez bin
'Abdullah Ar-Rajihi, and Muhammad Al-'Ali Al-Barrak (Riyadh, Kingdom of
Saudi Arabia: Darussalam, 2003)

'Imaduddeen Isma'eel ibn Katheer Al-Qurashi, *In Defence of the True Faith:
Battles, Expeditions, Peace Treaties and their Consequences in the life of Prophet
Muhammad*, trans. Research Department of Darussalam (Riyadh, Kingdom of
Saudi Arabia: Darussalam, 2010)

Abu 'Abd Allah Muhammad ibn Sa'd ibn Mani' al-Zuhri al-Basri, *Kitab al-
Tabaqat al-Kabir*, Vol. 2, trans. S. Moinul Haq (New Delhi, India: Kitab Bhavan,
2009)

623

The first Muslim military expedition took place in March 623. During the year of 623 there were a total of four expeditions (which include small raids), and four *Ghazwahs*, a term indicating a military expedition

---

Abu Ja'far Muhammad b. Jarir al-Tabari, *The History of al-Tabari: The Foundation of the Community*, Vol. VII, trans. M. V. McDonald and annotated W. Montgomery Watt (Albany, New York: State University of New York Press, 1987)

Abu Ja'far Muhammad b. Jarir al-Tabari, *The History of al-Tabari: The Last Years of the Prophet*, Vol. IX, trans. and annotated Ismail K. Poonawala (Albany, New York: State University of New York Press, 1990)

Abu Ja'far Muhammad b. Jarir al-Tabari, *The History of al-Tabari: The Victory of Islam*, Vol. VIII, trans. and annotated Michael Fishbein (Albany, New York: State University of New York Press, 1997)

Muhammad b. 'Umar al-Waqidi, *The Life of Muhammad: Al-Waqidi's Kitab al-Maghazi*, trans. Rizwi Faizer, Amal Ismail, and AbdulKader Tayob, ed. Rizwi Faizer, (London and New York: Routledge, 2013)

Muhammad ibn Ishaq, *The Life of Muhammad (Sirat Rasul Allah)*, trans. Alfred Guillaume (Karachi: Oxford University Press, 2007)

Ahmad ibn Yahya ibn Jabir Al-Baladhuri, *The Origins of the Islamic State, Being a Translation from the Arabic, Accompanied with Annotations, Geographic and Historic Notes of the Kitab Fituh Al-Buldan of Al-Imam Abu-L Abbas Ahmad Ibn-Jabir Al-Baladhuri*, trans. Philip Khuri Hitti (1916; rpt. Lexington, Kentucky: Ulan Press, 2014)

Safiur-Rahman Al-Mubarakpuri, *The Sealed Nectar* (Riyadh, Kingdom of Saudi Arabia: Darussalam, 2008) – a modern biography.

'Imaduddeen Isma'eel ibn Katheer Al-Qurashi, *Winning the Hearts and Souls: Expeditions and Delegations in the Lifetime of Prophet Muhammad*, trans. Research Department of Darussalam (Riyadh, Kingdom of Saudi Arabia: Darussalam, 2010)

personally led by Muhammad. There was no record of Muhammad having prohibited the killing of women and children in this year.

624

The year 624 started out with the Muslim victory at the Battle of Badr. Prior to this battle, Muhammad had forbidden the killing of certain individuals among the Quraysh (Meccan) warriors, including his uncle, and members of the Banu Hashim tribe who had not wanted to come to Badr. However, due to circumstances, including not being recognized in battle, some of the individuals were killed anyway.

In March Muhammad issued his first order to kill an individual when he had had enough of 'Asma' Bint Marwan, a poetess who used her poetry to insult him and to vilify Islam. Muhammad said, "Who will rid me of Marwan's daughter?"[41] A Muslim went in the middle of the night and killed 'Asma' with his sword while she was asleep and her children were lying asleep around her. When he was told about this, Muhammad said, "You have helped God and His apostle, O 'Umayr!"[42]

In April Muhammad dealt with Abu 'Afak, who was about 120 years old. Abu 'Afak had refused to become a Muslim and had ridiculed Muhammad after the battle of Badr.[43] Muhammad said, "Who will deal with this rascal for me?" One of the Muslims then went out and killed Abu 'Afak while he was sleeping.[44]

After the killing of Abu 'Afak, there were three *Ghazwahs* and one expedition. Then, around August or September, Muhammad decided to

---

[41]   *The Life of Muhammad*, p. 676.

[42]   Ibid.

[43]   *The Life of Muhammad: Al-Waqidi's Kitab al-Maghazi*, pp. 86-87.

[44]   *The Life of Muhammad*, p. 675.

deal with Ka'b bin Al-Ashraf, a Jewish poet in Medina who had criticized him and written poetry offensive to Muslim women:

> *Narrated Jabir bin 'Abdullah: Allah's Messenger said*
> *"Who will kill Ka'b bin Al-Ashraf who has hurt Allah and*
> *His Messenger?"[45]*

Some Muslims made a plan to kill Ka'b, and Muhammad then

> *sent them off and said: "March forth in the Name of*
> *Allah." And he said: "O Allah, help them," meaning the*
> *group that he sent to Ka'b bin al-Ashraf.[46]*

Ka'b was tricked into coming out of his fortress house and was killed by the Muslims. They cut off his head and gave it to Muhammad; Muhammad "praised Allah on his being slain."[47] The next morning, after Ka'b had been killed, Muhammad gave his Muslim followers a general order, "Whoever of the Jews falls into your hands, kill him."[48]

---

[45]   *Sahih Al-Bukhari*, Vol. 5, Book 64, No. 4037, p. 221.

[46]   Ahmad bin Muhammad bin Hanbal ash-Shaibani, *Musnad Imam Ahmad Bin Hanbal*, Vol. 2, trans. Nasiruddin Al-Khattab, ed. Huda Al-Khattab (Riyadh, Kingdom of Saudi Arabia: Darussalam, 2012), No. 2391, p. 442. A similar version of this statement was reported in *The History of al-Tabari: The Foundation of the Community*, p. 96; *The Life of Muhammad*, p. 368; and *Kitab al-Tabaqat al-Kabir*, Vol. 2, p. 36. For a general statement about Muhammad supplicating Allah for their success, see *The Sealed Nectar*, p. 288.

[47]   *Kitab al-Tabaqat al-Kabir*, Vol. 2, p. 37. It was similarly reported in *The Life of Muhammad: Al-Waqidi's Kitab al-Maghazi*, p. 95; and *The Sealed Nectar*, p. 289.

[48]   *The History of al-Tabari: The Foundation of the Community*, p. 97. This was similarly reported in *The Life of Muhammad*, p. 369 (*Kill any Jew that falls into your power*); and *Kitab al-Tabaqat al-Kabir*, Vol. 2, p. 37 (*Kill every Jew whom you come across*).

27

And Muhammad also stated that a similar fate would befall anyone who insulted him:

> *The Jews and the polytheists among them were alarmed.*
> *They came to the Prophet when it was morning and said,*
> *"Our companion, who was one of our lords, was knocked*
> *up at night and murdered treacherously with no crime or*
> *incident by him that we know of." The Messenger of God*
> *replied, "If he had remained as others of similar opinion*
> *remained he would not have been killed treacherously.*
> *But he hurt us and insulted us with poetry, and one does*
> *not do this among you, but he shall be put to the sword."[49]*

The year concluded with two more *Ghazwahs* and one more expedition.

Summary: In spite of the three murders ordered by Muhammad and the military actions, there was no record of Muhammad having prohibited the killing of women and children. In fact, in this year Muhammad had actually ordered the murder of a woman!

625

The first military action of 625 occurred in March when a Meccan army attacked Medina. This was the Battle of Uhud. Many of the Meccans brought their wives along to encourage them in their battle with the Muslims. When Muhammad was advised that the women were being brought along, he said,

> *The women desire to instigate the community and remind*
> *them of the dead of Badr.[50]*

---

[49]   *The Life of Muhammad: Al-Waqidi's Kitab al-Maghazi*, p. 96.

[50]   Ibid., p. 103. That Muhammad was advised of the women with the Meccan warriors was also noted in *Kitab al-Tabaqat al-Kabir*, Vol. 2, p. 43.

There is no record that Muhammad admonished his Muslim warriors not to kill any of these women.

On the day of the battle, Abu Dujana, one of the Muslim warriors, was given Muhammad's sword to use in the battle. Abu Dujana later stated that during the battle,

> *I saw a woman at that time inciting the people in a dreadful manner. I raised the sword above her for I did not consider her to be other than a man. He said: I hated that I struck a woman with the sword of the Messenger of God.*[51]

However, there were two Muslim scholars that said the woman was not killed; according to their writings, Abu Dujana explained why he had not killed the woman:

> *I respected the apostle's sword too much to use it on a woman.*[52]

So at the Battle of Uhud, a Muslim warrior either killed a woman with Muhammad's sword, or did not kill her, but only because he had too much respect for the sword to use it on a woman. There were no recorded comments from Muhammad about this incident either way.

The year 625 continued with one *Ghazwah* and three expeditions. Then in July, Muhammad told two Muslims to secretly go to Mecca and kill one of the Meccan leaders. They were unsuccessful. This was followed by a *Ghazwah* against one of the Jewish tribes in Medina, the Bani Nadir; the Jews were defeated and expelled from Medina.

---

[51]   *The Life of Muhammad: Al-Waqidi's Kitab al-Maghazi*, p. 127.

[52]   *The Life of Muhammad*, p. 375. This statement was similarly reported in *The History of al-Tabari: The Foundation of the Community*, pp. 116 and 138. It was repeated in the modern biography, *The Sealed Nectar*, p. 309.

The final military action of 625 was the *Ghazwah* of Dhat Al-Riqa'. Even though there was no fighting reported, a wife of a non-Muslim was somehow killed by one of the Muslims.[53] There were no recorded comments about this from Muhammad.

Summary: In the year 625 there were three *Ghazwahs* and four expeditions, with the wife of a non-Muslim killed in one of the *Ghazwahs*. In the Battle of Uhud, Muhammad knew that there were woman accompanying the Meccan warriors and it was possible that his sword had been used to kill a woman. Nevertheless, there was no record in this year of Muhammad having prohibited the killing of women and children.

626

In the year 626 there were only two *Ghazwahs*. In this year, as in the previous years, there was no record of Muhammad having prohibited the killing of women and children.

627

The year 627 started out with the Battle of the Trench (*Ghazwah of Al-Khandaq*) in February or March. An alliance of Meccans and other Arab tribes, totally 10,000 warriors, marched on Medina. The Muslims dug a protective trench and there was some minor fighting. The alliance soon crumbled, and its members returned to their respective lands.

Almost immediately after the Battle of the Trench, Muhammad besieged the Jewish Bani Qurayzah tribe. The Jews surrendered, and 600-900 males (all the males who had reached puberty) were beheaded. One woman was beheaded for reportedly having killed a Muslim by dropping a

---

[53]   *The History of al-Tabari: The Foundation of the Community*, p. 164; *The Life of Muhammad*, p. 447; *In Defence of the True Faith*, p. 165; and *Sunan Abu Dawud*, Vol. 1, No. 198, pp. 130-131.

millstone on him.[54] Here is an interesting explanation for why the rest of the women of the Bani Qurayzah and the children were spared:

> ...the reason why the children and women of Banu Quraythah were spared, was because there was a benefit [Maslahah] in keeping them alive – meaning enslavement. And killing them would have meant destroying valuable property. But as Az-Zayla'i (ra) clarifies – that if there is indeed a benefit in killing the women and children of the kuffar – a benefit which would have to be greater than the benefit of enslaving them – then it is permissible to kill them.[55]

---

[54] However, one modern commentary provided this explanation for why the woman was beheaded:

> It is said that the woman had verbally abused and insulted the Messenger of Allah.

Sunan Abu Dawud, Vol. 3, Comment to Hadith No. 2671, p. 297.

[55] Commentary in The Clarification Regarding Intentionally Targeting Women and Children, At-Tibyan Publications, October 31, 2004, n. 89, p. 37. Accessed on November 25, 2013 at

http://archive.org/details/IntentionalityTargetingWomenAndChildren.

This essay was one of two essays mentioned on p. 29 of the special Westgate Mall edition of Gaidi Mtaani. The mentioning of these essays was preceded by the following explanation:

> After the Westgate attack the Hypocrites, apologetic scholars and the media created an environment to confuse the Muslim Masses with much focus on 'killing the innocent' and 'killing women and children'. What is the Islamic ruling on these issues? Here are two books compiled by At-Tibyan publications from renown [sic] sincere Muslim scholars on these matters.

In April of 627, after four years of expeditions, *Ghazwahs*, battles, and directed killings, we have the first recorded incident of Muhammad prohibiting the killing of women and children. [56] This incident involved Muhammad sending a small group of Muslims to the house of Abu Rafi', a Jew who had criticized Muhammad. The Muslims were ordered to kill Abu Rafi', but before they left Muhammad "forbade them to kill women or children." [57] It was this command that prevented one of the Muslims

---

[56]   Muslim scholars differ about when this incident happened. I consulted six different biographies of Muhammad and found four different time periods for this occurrence between December 624 and January 628. Three of the biographies agreed on the time period of April 627 (see below); consequently, I am using this as the time frame for the murder of Abu Rafi':

Al-Tabari wrote that it happened around December 624 (Jumada al-Akhirah, 3 AH); see *The History of al-Tabari: The Foundation of the Community*, p. 100.

Al-Waqidi maintained it happen around May of 626 (Dhu l-Hijja, 4 AH); see *The Life of Muhammad: Al-Waqidi's Kitab al-Maghazi*, p. 192.

Ibn Ishaq wrote that it happened shortly after the defeat of the Bani Qurayzah, which would be around April 627 (Dhu l-Hijja, 5 AH); see *The Life of Muhammad*, p. 482. This was the time frame also pointed out by Ibn Kathir (*In Defence of the True Faith*, p. 212); and repeated in *The Sealed Nectar*, p. 381.

Ibn Sa'd wrote that it happened around January 628 (Ramadan, 6 AH); see *Kitab al-Tabaqat al-Kabir*, Vol. 2, p. 112.

[57]   *The History of al-Tabari: The Foundation of the Community*, p. 102; this statement was also quoted in *The Life of Muhammad*, p. 482. This prohibition was also noted in *Al-Muwatta of Imam Malik ibn Anas*, 21.3.8; and the modern biography *The Sealed Nectar*, p. 380.

It is interesting to note that two authoritative biographies of Muhammad made no mention of, or reference to, this prohibition of killing women and children when discussing the murder of Abu Rafi': *In Defence of the True Faith*, pp. 212-214; and *Kitab al-Tabaqat al-Kabir*, Vol. 2, pp. 112-113.

from killing the wife of Abu Rafi', who was shrieking as she watched her husband being killed by Muslim swords.[58]

However, the next month, Muhammad sent a Muslim warrior, 'Abdullah b. Unays, to kill Sufyan b. Khalid. 'Abdullah befriended Sufyan, joined him in his tent, and then killed him; he cut off Sufyan's head, "leaving his women crying over him." 'Abdullah brought Sufyan's head back to Muhammad, and Muhammad praised 'Abdullah.[59]

From June through November there were two *Ghazwahs* and nine expeditions. In December Muhammad led the *Ghazwah* to al-Muraysi' and attacked the Bani al-Mustaliq tribe. The tribe was defeated and their women and children were divided among the Muslims. Al-Shafi'i, a Muslim scholar and founder of one of the major schools of Sharia Law, described a portion of the battle:

> *The Prophet launched a raid against the tribe of al-Mustalaq and they fought back. So he commanded to set fire to their fortifications all night long with the widespread knowledge that women and children were in there. This was because it was an idolatrous camp, not exempt [from raiding]. Instead, it was the intentional killing of children and women that was prohibited, whom the Prophet [preferred to] trade and treat as property.[60]*

There was also no mention of this prohibition when the killing of Abu Rafi' was reported in *Sahih Al-Bukhari*: Vol. 4, Book 56, Nos. 3022-3023, pp. 162-163; and Vol. 5, Book 64, Chapter 16, pp. 223-227.

[58]   *The History of al-Tabari: The Foundation of the Community*, pp. 102 and 104; *The Life of Muhammad*, p. 483; *The Life of Muhammad: Al-Waqidi's Kitab al-Maghazi*, p. 192; and *Al-Muwatta of Imam Malik ibn Anas*, 21.3.8.

[59]   *The Life of Muhammad: Al-Waqidi's Kitab al-Maghazi*, p. 262. This was also reported in *Kitab al-Tabaqat al-Kabir*, Vol. 2, pp. 60-61.

[60]   *The Al Qaeda Reader*, trans. and ed. Raymond Ibrahim, (New York: Broadway Books, 2007), p. 167.

That same month, Muhammad sent a raiding party to Dumat al-Jandal to "invite" the people to become Muslims. Before the raiding party left, Muhammad ordered,

> ...fight everyone in the way of God and kill those who disbelieve in God. Do not be deceitful with the spoil; do not be treacherous, nor mutilate, nor kill children. This is God's ordinance and the practice of his prophet among you.[61]

But it is interesting to point out that there were variations in what Muhammad supposedly said in this particular incident. In the version below Muhammad only prohibited the killing of "a boy" (which raises the question about the permissibility of killing a girl):

> Attack in the name of God, and in the way of God and fight those who disbelieve in God. Do not be an extremist, double cross anyone or kill a boy.[62]

And in another version, Muhammad only prohibited the killing of a newborn child (*Walid*):

> In the name of Allah and in the way of Allah fight him who believes not in Allah, do not defraud, do not deceive, and do not kill Walid.[63]

The differing reports about Muhammad's command apparently did not become an issue because the tribe "accepted" Islam. But there was no report that he specifically forbad the killing of women in this expedition.

The year closed with two more expeditions.

---

[61]   *The Life of Muhammad*, p. 672.

[62]   *The Life of Muhammad: Al-Waqidi's Kitab al-Maghazi*, p. 275.

[63]   *Kitab al-Tabaqat al-Kabir*, Vol. 2, p. 110.

34

Summary: 627 was a busy year not only in terms of Muslim military actions, but also in terms of addressing the issue of Muhammad's commands not to kill women and children. The year started out with a battle and then the siege of a Jewish tribe. And only after these do we find the first recorded incident of Muhammad prohibiting the killing of women and children, when he ordered the murder of Abu Rafi'. This incident was followed by the killing of a man inside his tent, with his wives in the area, and eleven *Ghazwahs* and expeditions, all with no mention of a prohibition against killing women and children. Then Muhammad led an attack on the Bani al-Mustaliq in which the Muslims intentionally set fire to the fortifications, knowing there were women and children inside. This was followed by an expedition dispatched by Muhammad with varied reports about whom he prohibited from being killed; the only aspect agreed on was that Muhammad did not mention the killing of women among these prohibitions. The year ended with two more expeditions, with no comments from Muhammad about the killing of women and children.

628

The year 628 started out with the Expedition to Wadi al-Qura in January, led by Zayd bin Harithah. The raiding party fought against and took captives from the Bani Fazarah tribe. Among the captives was an old woman named Umm Qirfah. She met a cruel fate:

> *Zayd b. Harithah ordered Qays to kill Umm Qirfah, and he killed her cruelly. He tied each of her legs with a rope and tied the ropes to two camels, and they split her in two.*[64]

There was no recorded comment from Muhammad about this intentionally cruel killing of a woman. This should not be surprising when we consider Zayd's background. Muhammad's first wife Khadija had originally given

---

[64]   *The History of al-Tabari: The Victory of Islam*, p. 96. The same story is related in *The Life of Muhammad*, p. 665. That Umm Qirfah was killed in this manner is also mentioned in *The Life of Muhammad: Al-Waqidi's Kitab al-Maghazi*, p. 278; and *Kitab al-Tabaqat al-Kabir*, Vol. 2, p. 112.

Zayd to Muhammad as a slave. Muhammad subsequently freed Zayd and adopted him as his son. Zayd was beloved and trusted by Muhammad and was often placed in command of Muslim military expeditions. Therefore, if Muhammad had already issued a general prohibition against the killing of women, Zayd would have known about it and he would not have ordered Umm Qirfah to be killed.

The killing of Umm Qirfah was followed by two expeditions.

In March the Treaty of al-Hudaybiyah was signed between Muhammad and the Quraysh tribe (of Mecca). This came about because Muhammad, accompanied by about 1,400 Muslims, had travelled to Mecca to perform the "lesser pilgrimage" and visit the Ka'bah. The Meccans did not want the Muslims to enter Mecca and sent a force against them. Muhammad evaded the force and camped at al-Hudaybiyah, making no effort to enter Mecca. This resulted in a treaty between Muhammad and the Quraysh that, among other things, guaranteed a ten year peace between them (although the treaty only lasted less than two years).

This incident is important for two reasons. In the first place, this is the first report of Muhammad being asked about killing the women and children of the enemy (polytheists):

> *It is reported on the authority of Sa'b b. Jathama that the*
> *Prophet of Allah (may peace be upon him), when asked*
> *about the women and children of the polytheists being*
> *killed during the night raid, said: They are from them.*[65]

---

[65]   *Sahih Muslim*, Vol. 5, No. 1745, p. 167. For other reports and variations on Muhammad's response, see *Sahih Al-Bukhari*, Vol. 4, Book 56, No. 3012, pp. 157-158 (*They are from them*); *Jami' At-Tirmidhi*, Vol. 3, No. 1570, pp. 342-343 (*They are from their fathers*); *Sunan Abu Dawud*, Vol. 3, No. 2672, p. 297 (*They are from them*); and *Sunan Ibn Majah*, Vol. 4, No. 2839, p. 88 (*They are from among them*).

Al-Waqidi reported a variation on Muhammad's response to Sa'b b. Jathama that pertained only to children:

So Muhammad said it was permissible to kill women and children during an attack, not only because they too were polytheists, but also because it could be difficult to distinguish among the enemy during a raid in darkness.

In the second place, Muhammad had an interesting reaction when faced with the possibility of armed resistance to keep the Muslims from entering Mecca and going to the Ka'bah. Muhammad was advised that some of the Quraysh (*Quraish*) who wanted to stop the Muslims were camped at a place named Baldah, and they had their women and children with them. Muhammad turned to his followers with an interesting question:

> *The Prophet proceeded on till he reached (a village called) Ghadir-al-Ashtat. There his spy came and said, "The Quraish (infidels) have collected a great number of people against you, and they have collected against you the Ethiopians, and they will fight with you, and will stop you and prevent you from entering the Ka'bah." The Prophet said, "O people! Give me your opinion. Do you recommend that I should destroy the families and offspring of those who want to stop us from (going to) the Ka'bah?"*[66]

Here we have Muhammad asking the Muslims if they should intentionally "destroy" the women and children of the Quraysh. As it turned out, the

---

> *"O Messenger of God, what is the opinion when we come upon the enemy and the attack takes place in the darkness of dawn, and we mistakenly strike children hiding under the bellies of the horses?" The Messenger of God said, "They are with their parents." He [Sa'b] said: I heard him say, at that time, "There is no protection except for God and his Messenger."*

The Life of Muhammad: Al-Waqidi's Kitab al-Maghazi, p. 283.

[66] *Sahih Al-Bukhari*, Vol. 5, Book 64, Nos. 4178-4179, p. 303.

37

Muslims decided to sign a treaty instead of killing those women and children.

So in the events leading up to the signing of the Treaty of al-Hudaybiyah we have Muhammad first saying it was permissible to kill women and children of the enemy because they too were polytheists and could be considered as collateral damage of an attack, and then suggesting the idea of intentionally attacking and killing the women and children of the enemy. These statements undermine any claim that there had been a doctrinal, general prohibition against the killing of women and children prior to this time.

To further support the idea that there had been no such doctrinal, general prohibition, Shaykh 'Abdul-'Aziz Al-Jarbu made a crucial observation with regard to Muhammad asking his Muslim warriors about attacking these families:

> *And indeed the Messenger of Allah is far removed from asking advise from his Companions regarding something which was prohibited upon him…Nay, rather he wouldn't seek advice on anything except that which was made permissible for him.*[67]

This Muslim scholar makes the important point that Muhammad would never seek advice on something that had already been *prohibited upon him*. Consequently, even up to the time of the signing of the Treaty of al-Hudaybiyah, there was no general prohibition against the killing of women and children.

In June, Muhammad led a Muslim army against the Jewish community of Khaybar. Muhammad set the tone when he told his warriors,

---

[67]   *The Clarification Regarding Intentionally Targetting Women and Children*, p. 17.

*You will not go out with me unless you desire jihad. As
for plunder, there will be none.*[68]

Khaybar consisted of a number of Jewish fortresses. The Muslims
conquered, and then obtained a mangonel (catapult) from the Jewish
fortress of al-Nata. They put it together and used it to throw stones against
the fortress of al-Shiqq; Muhammad had earlier been advised that this was
one of the locations to which the children of al-Nata had been sent. The
Muslims obtained another mangonel after conquering the fortress of al-
Sa'b b. Mu'adh. The Muslims used mangonels against the fortress of al-
Nizar, which the Jews had considered a safe place for their women and
children to stay. The Muslims also used the mangonel against the fortress
of al-Katiba.[69] There were no recorded comments from Muhammad about
the possibility of killing women and children by using the mangonels.

The attack on Khaybar was followed by two expeditions.

Then, in December, Abu Bakr, Muhammad's father-in-law and trusted
friend, led a Muslim raiding party to Najd. Their battle cry was *Amit!
Amit!* [Kill! Kill!].[70] Salamah bin Akwa', one of the participants in the
raid, described what happened:

> *It was narrated from Iyas bin Salamah bin Akwa', that his
> father said: "We attacked Hawazin, with Abu Bakr,
> during the time of the Prophet, and we arrived at an oasis
> belonging to Bani Fazarah during the last part of the*

---

[68]   *The Life of Muhammad: Al-Waqidi's Kitab al-Maghazi*, p. 312. A similar
statement by Muhammad was reported in *Kitab al-Tabaqat al-Kabir*, Vol. 2, p.
132.

[69]   *The Life of Muhammad: Al-Waqidi's Kitab al-Maghazi*, pp. 318-319,
327, and 330; and *The Sealed Nectar*, p. 438.

[70]   *The Life of Muhammad: Al-Waqidi's Kitab al-Maghazi*, p. 355; *Sunan
Abu Dawud*, Vol. 3, No. 2638, pp. 275-276; and *Kitab al-Tabaqat al-Kabir*, Vol.
2, p. 146.

*night. We attacked at dawn, raiding the people of the
oasis, and killed them, nine or seven households.* [71]

Salamah stated, "I slew with my hand members of seven families of the
polytheists."[72]

Abu Bakr was Muhammad's father-in-law and trusted friend. Had the
killing of women and children been prohibited, Abu Bakr would never
have allowed "nine or seven households" of people to be killed.

It was later said that there had not been "an expedition quicker in return or
greater in spoils than this expedition."[73] There was also no recorded
comment from Muhammad about the killing of *nine or seven households*
and *members of seven families*.

The year 628 ended with another expedition.

Summary: 628 was an interesting year in terms of our subject. The year
started with an expedition in which a trusted Muslim commander ordered
an old woman to be killed; and he allowed her to be killed by tying her
legs to two camels and then being split in two. During the events leading
to the signing of the Treaty of al-Hudaybiyah, Muhammad said it was
permissible to kill women and children of the non-Muslims because "they
are from them." And then he actually suggested that the Muslims
"destroy" the women and children of those warriors opposing them. In
June, Muhammad led an attack against the Jewish fortresses of Khaybar;
the Muslims used catapults against those fortresses, knowing that there

---

[71]   *Sunan Ibn Majah*, Vol. 4, No. 2840, pp. 88-89.

[72]   *Kitab al-Tabaqat al-Kabir*, Vol. 2, p. 146. For additional statements
from Salamah claiming that he had personally killed a total of seven people, see
Sunan Abu Dawud, Vol. 3, No. 2638, pp. 275-276 (*I killed seven idolators in their
homes*); and *The Life of Muhammad: Al-Waqidi's Kitab al-Maghazi*, p. 355 (*I
killed seven of the people*).

[73]   *Jami' At-Tirmidhi*, Vol. 6, No. 3561, p. 267.

were women and children in some of them. Then at the end of the year, Abu Bakr led a raiding party to Najd, in which the Muslims killed *nine or seven households*. Any supposed general prohibition against the killing of women and children was certainly not applicable in 628.

629

The year 629 started out with six expeditions. Then around August or September, Muhammad sent a force of 3,000 Muslims to Mu'ta. Muhammad prohibited the killing of women, children, and suckling children.[74] This was followed by three more expeditions.

Then in November Muhammad sent an expedition to Khadira. He told his warriors, "Make an attack, but do not kill women and children."[75] The year ended with another expedition.

Summary: 629 was an interesting year because we have two expeditions where Muhammad specifically prohibited the killing of women and children, with no variations or conflicting orders. However, there were also ten expeditions interspersed around them that year in which there is no record of Muhammad having issued a similar prohibition.

630

630 started out with the Muslim conquest of Mecca in January. As the Muslims were approaching Mecca, Muhammad ordered the killing of

---

[74]   *The Life of Muhammad: Al-Waqidi's Kitab al-Maghazi*, pp. 372-373. In *The Sealed Nectar*, we find that Muhammad told his warriors,

   kill no children or woman, nor an ageing man or a hermit be killed...

The Sealed Nectar, p. 453.

[75]   *The Life of Muhammad: Al-Waqidi's Kitab al-Maghazi*, p. 383.

certain men and women in Mecca. Some of those targeted saved themselves by converting to Islam before they could be killed. However, some of the women were reported to have been killed before they could convert.

After the conquest of Mecca, Muhammad sent two expeditions, totaling 500 warriors, to different areas with the general command "to attack those who were not following Islam."[76] Other than that qualification, there were no stated restrictions about whom to attack.

Muhammad also sent two Muslim forces out, each one to destroy the statue of a pagan goddess. At the site of the goddess *al'Uzza*, the Muslim leader killed an unarmed black woman who approached him; Muhammad later rationalized this killing by saying that she was actually *al'Uzza*. At the site of the goddess *Manat*, the respective Muslim leader killed another unarmed black woman who had approached him. There was no comment from Muhammad.

At that same time, Muhammad sent an expedition under the leadership of Khalid bin al-Walid to invite the Bani Jadhima to Islam. Muhammad gave them a general command to kill anyone who was not a Muslim:

> *Al-'Abbas Ibn al-Fadl informed us, Sufyan Ibn 'Uyaynah informed us: 'Abd al-Malik Ibn Nawfal Ibn Musahiq al-Qurashi related to me on the authority of his father; he said: The Apostle of Allah, may Allah bless him, sent us on the day of Nakhlah (when al'Uzza was demolished), and said: Slay the people as long as you do not hear a mu'adhdhin* [one who calls Muslims to prayer] *or see a mosque.*[77]

When the Muslims approached them, the Bani Jadhima said they were already Muslims and laid down their weapons. Khalid distrusted their

---

76   Ibid., p. 429.

77   *Kitab al-Tabaqat al-Kabir*, Vol. 2, p. 184.

claim, and the Muslims bound them. The next morning many of them were beheaded by the Muslims.

One of those captives had been allowed to first speak with a woman, and then he was beheaded. The woman then

> went up to him when he was beheaded, and she threw herself down on him and kept kissing him until she died beside him.[78]

Since it is doubtful that the Muslims returned sometime later to find the woman dead from dehydration or starvation, this narration tells us that the Muslims killed the woman.

When Muhammad found out that many of the Bani Jadhima men had been beheaded even though, as it turned out, they had actually earlier accepted Islam, he was upset with Khalid and sent a Muslim to pay the blood money for those killed. There is no record that Muhammad said anything specifically about the killing of the woman.

Toward the end of January Muhammad led a force of 12,000 Muslims against the Hawazin and Thaqif tribes, who had banded together to attack Mecca. These two tribes had brought their women and children with them. When Muhammad was advised of this before the battle, he said,

> That will be the plunder of the Muslims tomorrow, God willing![79]

---

[78] *The History of al-Tabari: The Victory of Islam*, p. 192. That the lady was kissing the beheaded man until she also died was reported in *The Life of Muhammad: Al-Waqidi's Kitab al-Maghazi*, p. 432; *Kitab al-Tabaqat al-Kabir*, Vol. 2, p. 185; and *The Life of Muhammad*, p. 564.

[79] *The Life of Muhammad: Al-Waqidi's Kitab al-Maghazi*, p. 439. A similar statement by Muhammad was reported in *Winning the Hearts and Souls*, p. 74 (*booty*); *Sunan Abu Dawud*, Vol. 3, No. 2501, p. 204 (*spoils*); and *The Sealed Nectar*, p. 477 (*spoils*).

The battle occurred in the valley of Hunayn. The Muslims were initially put to flight, but they were able to rally and began to furiously fight the enemy. The Muslims also began to kill the children of the enemy. When Muhammad was advised of this, he probably realized they were only following his initial orders, and he put a stop to the killing of the children:

> *Then the Apostle of Allah, may Allah bless him, ordered*
> *them to kill whom they could. Thereupon the Muslims*
> *grew furious and killed them and also began to kill their*
> *children. It (report) reached the Apostle of Allah, may*
> *Allah bless him, and he stopped them from killing the*
> *children.*[80]

After the Muslim victory at Hunayn, they began moving toward the fortress of al-Ta'if, with Khalid bin al-Walid commanding the vanguard. It was during this time that the following incident happened:

> *Ibn 'Umar narrated that a woman was found killed in one*
> *of the expeditions of the Messenger of Allah, so the*
> *Messenger of Allah rebuked that, and he prohibited killing*
> *women and children.*[81]

---

[80]   *Kitab al-Tabaqat al-Kabir*, Vol. 2, p. 187. That the Muslims were killing children until Muhammad ordered it to be stopped was also reported in *The Life of Muhammad: Al-Waqidi's Kitab al-Maghazi*, p. 444.

[81]   *Jami' At-Tirmidhi*, Vol. 3, No. 1569, pp. 341-342. For similar *hadiths* in which Muhammad forbad the killing of women and children at this time, see *Sahih Muslim*, Vol. 5, Nos. 1744-1744R1, p. 167; *Sunan Ibn Majah*, Vol. 4, No. 2841, p. 89; and *Sunan Abu Dawud*, Vol. 3, No. 2668, p. 295.

It is interesting to note that there are variations of this *hadith* with different prohibitions by Muhammad:

Tell Khalid: "Do not kill a woman or a hired hand."
     Sunan Abu Dawud, Vol. 3, No. 2669, p. 295.

Go to Khalid bin Walid...Do not kill any women or any (farm) laborer.
     Sunan Ibn Majah, Vol. 4, No. 2842, p. 89.

But Muhammad's prohibition against killing women and children was not a general prohibition. Because, after sending a force to Awtas, Muhammad led his Muslim army in a siege of the fortress at al-Ta'if. The siege lasted 14-19 days, and catapults were used against the fortress. Al-Jassa, a later Muslim scholar, made an interesting observation:

> *But the biographers relay that the Prophet besieged the inhabitants of Ta'if and fired at them with catapults, despite his ban on killing women and children. He did so knowing full well that women and children would be struck, for it was not possible to differentiate between them.*[82]

During 630 there were seven more expeditions and the *Ghazwah* of Tabuk.

The *Ghazwah* of Tabuk occurred in October, when Muhammad led an army of 30,000 Muslims against the Byzantines in the area of Tabuk. There was no fighting. But it was the preparation for this military action that was significant. There was initially opposition to this military action among some of the Muslims (who were referred to as "the hypocrites"). Some of them were trying to dissuade other Muslims from participating. When Muhammad heard about this and where some of them were gathering, the following took place:

> *A trustworthy person told me on the authority of Muhammad b. Talha b. 'Abdu'l-Rahman from Ishaq b.*

..he sent word to Khalid and forbade him to kill child, or woman, or hired slave.
The Life of Muhammad, p. 576.

"Catch up with Khalid and inform him not to kill children and slaves."
Winning the Hearts and Souls, p. 90.

"Surely the Messenger of God forbade you to kill women and old men."
The Life of Muhammad: Al-Waqidi's Kitab al-Maghazi, p. 448.

[82]   *The Al Qaeda Reader*, p. 165.

Ibrahim b. 'Abdullah b. Haritha from his father from his grandfather: The apostle heard that the hypocrites were assembling in the house of Suwaylim the Jew (his house was by Jasum) keeping men back from the apostle in the raid on Tabuk. So the prophet sent Talha b. 'Ubaydullah with a number of his friends to them with orders to burn Suwaylim's house down on them. Talha did so, and al-Dahhak b. Khalifa threw himself from the top of the house and broke his leg, and his friends rushed out and escaped.[83]

So Muhammad sent a group of Muslims to burn a house down on some men who were gathered inside it; there was no admonition about looking out for any women and children who might also be in that house.

Summary: In spite of Muhammad's previous injunctions against the killing of women and children, the year 630 started out with some women targeted for death when the Muslims conquered Mecca. Immediately after that conquest, Muslim expeditions were sent out with the general, unrestricted command to attack those who were not following Islam. Pagan shrines were destroyed and unarmed women were killed. Muhammad sent an expedition against the Bani Jadhima with the command to kill any non-Muslim, and a woman was killed as she was kissing her beheaded lover. During the battle at Hunayn the Muslims intentionally killed the children of the enemy until Muhammad ordered them to stop. Then, as he led the Muslims on the way to besiege al-Ta'if, Muhammad saw a dead woman and again ordered that woman and children were not to be killed. The Muslims then arrived at al-Ta'if and used catapults against the fortress, knowing that women and children were inside. This was followed by six expeditions. Then, while preparing for the *Ghazwah* of Tabuk, Muhammad ordered an occupied house in a suburb of Medina to be burned down around its occupants. There was then a final expedition in 630. From the siege of al-Ta'if in late January until the end

---

[83]   *The Life of Muhammad*, n. 858, p. 782.

of that year, there was no record that Muhammad said anything about the killing of women and children.

631

The year 631 saw a lessening in Muslim military activity, largely because after the conquest of Mecca the Arab tribes saw the strength of the Muslims and decided it was time to accept Islam. Nevertheless, there were four expeditions that year. The fourth expedition was sent to destroy Dhul-Khalas, a pagan shrine in Yemen. Jarir bin 'Abdullah, the commander of that expedition, later explained what they did there and Muhammad's reaction:

> *So, I set out with one hundred and fifty riders, and we dismantled it and killed whoever was present there. Then I came to the Prophet and informed him, and he invoked good upon us...*[84]

There was no record of Muhammad inquiring about the status of any women or children who might have been "present there."

632

Muhammad died on June 7, 632. However, in May he had ordered an expedition to attack the Byzantines at a town named Ubna (known as the Expedition to Mu'ta). Muhammad chose Usama ibn Zayd ibn Harithah to lead the expedition. Muhammad ordered Usama,

> *O Usama, attack in the name of God and in the path of God, and fight those who do not believe in God. Attack, but do not act treacherously. Do not kill a new born or a woman, and do not desire to meet the enemy, for indeed*

---

[84]   *Sahih Al-Bukhari*, Vol. 5, Book 64, No. 4355, p. 390.

you do not know whether you would be destroyed by
them...Know that Paradise is under the flashing gleam.[85]

---

[85]   *The Life of Muhammad: Al-Waqidi's Kitab al-Maghazi*, p. 546. "[U]nder
the flashing gleam" refers to the light reflecting on swords being wielded in battle.

One might hear the argument that Muhammad's admonition *do not desire to meet
the enemy* supports the claim that he generally cautioned his Muslim warriors
against fighting non-Muslims; i.e. *Jihad* was some kind of aberration in the early
days of Islam. However, this claim is effective only if the statement is taken out
of context. The above quote shows that the context for this admonition is that the
Muslims should be cautious and not overly confident because they might be
destroyed by that enemy. But *Jihad* was not to be generally avoided, because
Muhammad assured Usama that Paradise would be attained by wielding swords
and dying in the cause of Allah.

Another example of a similar statement by Muhammad is found in *Sahih Al-
Bukhari*:

> *Allah's Messenger during some of his holy battles waited till the
> sun had declined. And then he (Allah's Messenger) got up
> among the people and said, "O people! Do not wish to meet the
> enemy (in a battle) and ask Allah to save you (from calamities),
> but if you should meet the enemy, then be patient and let it be
> known to you that Paradise is under the shades of swords.*

Sahih Al-Bukhari, Vol. 4, Book 56, Nos. 2965-2966, p. 134; for a similar *hadith*
see *Sahih Muslim* Vol. 5, No. 1742, p. 166 (*...do not wish for an encounter with
the enemy...Paradise is under the shadows of the swords.*).

The above *hadith* in *Sahih Al-Bukhari* was explained, with the same emphasis on
the context, in a piece titled *Essay Regarding the Basic Rule of the Blood, Wealth
and Honour of the Disbelievers*:

> "*So the fact that he* [Muhammad] *said this Hadith while
> heading towards the fighting and the fact that he incited (his
> companions) upon the fighting in the very same Hadith,
> indicates that the forbiddance of wishing to meet the enemy is
> not in absolute terms and that it was merely from a specific
> point. And that is the warning against being satisfied and being
> overconfident with strength. And it is what Ibn Hajar pointed to*

48

But it was also reported that Muhammad said the following to Usama:

> *I have appointed you commander of this army. Attack the people of Ubna early in the morning and set fire (to their camp).*[86]

Muhammad's death on June 7th delayed the attack. Soon afterward, when Usama led his force to Ubna, he said,

---

> *in his explanation of this Hadith. He said: 'He only forbid the wishing to meet the enemy due to what is in that from the state of being pleased and having trust upon the self and being sure of the strength and underestimating the enemy. And all of this contradicts the being cautious and having determination. And it is said: "This forbiddance is held when doubt exists about the benefits or the possibility of harm. Otherwise, the fighting is a virtue and an obedience."*

Essay Regarding the Basic Rule of the Blood, Wealth and Honour of the Disbelievers, At-Tibyan Publications, August 22, 2004, pp. 42-43. Available at: http://islamicline.com/islamicbooks/Essay_Regarding_the_Basic_Asl_of_the_Blood,_Wealth_%20and_Honor_of_Kafireen-editable(www.islamicline.com).pdf. Accessed on November 25, 2013.

This essay was one of two mentioned on p. 29 of the special Westgate Mall edition of *Gaidi Mtaani*. The mentioning of these essays was preceded by the following explanation:

> *After the Westgate attack the Hypocrites, apologetic scholars and the media created an environment to confuse the Muslim Masses with much focus on 'killing the innocent' and 'killing women and children'. What is the Islamic ruling on these issues? Here are two books compiled by At-Tibyan publications from renown [sic] sincere Muslim scholars on these matters.*

[86] *Kitab al-Tabaqat al-Kabir*, Vol. 2, p. 235. Muhammad's command to attack in the morning and "burn" Ubna is also found in *Sunan Abu Dawud*, Vol. 3, No. 2616, p. 265; and *Sunan Ibn Majah*, Vol. 4, No. 2843, p. 90.

But the Messenger of God commanded me and this was
his last command to me: To hasten the march and to be
ahead of the news. And to raid them, without inviting
them [to Islam], *and to destroy and burn.*[87]

Usama obeyed that command:

He attacked them and their watch-word was: ya Mansur
Amit [O victorious one, kill]. *He killed him who met him,*
enslaved him whom he could, set fire to their boats, and
burnt their dwellings, farms and palm-groves which
turned into whirl-wind [sic] *of smoke. He drove his*
horses into their plains.[88]

So with the last expedition he dispatched, Muhammad initially told the
commander not to kill women and newborn children, but Muhammad then
gave a final command to indiscriminately "destroy and burn." His final
command was obeyed.

---

[87]   *The Life of Muhammad: Al-Waqidi's Kitab al-Maghazi*, p. 549.

[88]   *Kitab al-Tabaqat al-Kabir*, Vol. 2, p. 237. Al-Waqidi provided a similar
description:

When Usama reached Ubna and could see it with his eyes, he
mobilized his companions and said, "Go and raid...draw your
sword and place it in whoever confronts you." Then he pushed
them into the raid. A dog did not bark, and no one moved. The
enemy did not know except when the army attacked them calling
out their slogan, "O Mansur, Kill!" He killed those who
confronted him and took prisoner those he defeated. He set the
borders on fire and their houses and fields and date palm on
fire.

The Life of Muhammad: Al-Waqidi's Kitab al-Maghazi, p. 549.

Conclusion

The Muslim military actions started in March 623. Over the next four years Muhammad sent out 10 expeditions and led 15 *Ghazwahs*. During one of the *Ghazwahs* the wife of a non-Muslim was killed even though there was no reported battle; in another *Ghazwah*, a woman was beheaded for reportedly dropping a millstone on the head of a Muslim warrior, although there was another report that she had simply insulted Muhammad. Muhammad had three individuals killed, including a female poet; these individuals were all killed at their own homes, either with family around or the potential for family to be around. He ordered an unsuccessful attempt to kill another individual. He led the Muslims in three battles. In the Battle of Badr he prohibited the killing of certain enemy warriors. In the Battle of Uhud the enemy brought some women to encourage them in fighting. And during this battle a Muslim warrior was given Muhammad's sword to use; the warrior either killed a woman with it or had too much respect for the sword to use it on a woman. During this four year period there was no record of Muhammad prohibiting the killing of women and children.

The first report of a prohibition against the killing of women and children comes in April 627, when Muhammad ordered the killing of Abu Rafi'. However, the next month, on Muhammad's orders, Sufyan b. Khalid was killed in his tent, with his wives in the area. This was followed by nine expeditions and two *Ghazwahs*. In December 627 Muhammad led the *Ghazwah* to al-Muraysi'; after meeting resistance, Muhammad ordered that the fortifications be burned all night long, knowing that women and children were inside. And in that same month Muhammad sent out three expeditions. In only one, to Dumat al-Jandal, was there a record that Muhammad prohibited the killing of boys, or children.

In January 628 Muhammad sent an expedition to Wadi al-Qura under the leadership of his adopted son, Zayd bin Harithah; during this expedition Zayd ordered the killing of one of the captives, an old woman named Umm Qirfah. This was followed by two expeditions the next month. In March, prior to signing the Treaty of al-Hudaybiyah, Muhammad said it was permissible to kill the women and children of the enemy because they were from the enemy. During this same time period Muhammad proposed to his Muslim warriors that they attack and destroy the women and children of the enemy. This was followed by the *Ghazwah* to Khaybar in which catapults were used against the fortifications even though the Muslims knew there were women and children in some of them. There were four expeditions in the rest of 628; in one of them, the Expedition of Abu Bakr to Najd, the Muslims killed *nine or seven households*. There was no record of Muhammad prohibiting the killing of women and children during 628.

629 started out with six expeditions. Then in August or September, Muhammad sent an expedition to Mu'ta; he commanded them not to kill women and children. This was followed by three expeditions. Then there was the Expedition to Khadira, in which Muhammad prohibited the killing of women and children. This was followed by one more expedition in 629, with no mention about the killing of women and children.

In January 630 the Muslims conquered Mecca. Muhammad had ordered that certain people were to be killed, including a number of women. This conquest was followed by two expeditions sent out with general orders to attack anyone not following Islam. There were also three expeditions in which a woman was killed in each. Muhammad then led the *Ghazwah* against Hunayn; in the early part of the battle the Muslims intentionally killed the children of the enemy until Muhammad stopped them. Later, on seeing the body of a dead woman, Muhammad prohibited the killing of women and children. Then came another expedition and the siege of al-Ta'if; catapults were used against al-Ta'if even though the Muslims knew there were women and children inside. During the rest of 630 there were seven expeditions and the *Ghazwah* of Tabuk. While preparing for this *Ghazwah*, Muhammad ordered a house to be burned down around its occupants in a suburb of Medina. There was no admonition regarding the possibility of women and children being inside the house.

In 631 there were four expeditions. In one, the Expedition to Dhul-Khalas, the Muslims *killed whoever was present there*, and Muhammad "invoked good" on them for what they had done.

In 632 Muhammad commanded that an expedition be sent to Mu'ta. He originally told the commander of that expedition not to kill a newborn or a woman. But according to the commander, Muhammad's final command to him was to attack early in the morning, and *to destroy and burn.*

The vast majority of military actions during the life of Muhammad showed no record of Muhammad having prohibited the killing of women and children. The few times that he did issue such prohibitions in military actions were interspersed with the targeting of individual women for killing, and with military actions in which women and/or children were among the targets of attack.

The historical record shows that instead of it being a general, all-encompassing command issued by Muhammad to every Muslim military leader, and a part of Islamic doctrine, the prohibition against the killing of women and children was a specific, situational prohibition based on Muhammad's judgments and the demands of battle at the time (see *Appendix 4* for a chronological summary).

And in terms of killing women, there are two specific *hadiths* showing that Muhammad had no problem with the killing of women who criticized him:

1.   *It was narrated that 'Ikrimah said: "Ibn 'Abbas told us that a blind man had a female slave who had borne him a child (Umm Walad* [89]*) who reviled the Prophet and disparaged him, and he told her not to do that, but she did not stop, and he rebuked her, but she paid no heed. One night she started to disparage and revile the Prophet, so he took a dagger and put it in her stomach and pressed on it and killed her. There fell between her legs a child who was smeared with the blood that was there. The next morning mention of that was made to the Prophet and he assembled the people and said: 'By Allah, I adjure the man who did this, to stand up.' The blind man stood up and came through the people,*

---

[89]   *Umm* is the Arabic word for mother or "mother of." *Umm Walad* is a slave concubine who has born a child to her master.

trembling, and he came and sat before the Prophet. He said: 'O Messenger of Allah, I am the one who did it. She used to revile you and disparage you, and I told her not to do it, but she did not stop, and I rebuked her, but she paid no heed. I have two sons from her who are like two pearls, and she was good to me. Last night she started to revile you and disparage you, and I took a dagger and placed it on her stomach and I pressed on it until I killed her.' The Prophet said: 'Bear witness that no retaliation is due for her blood.'[90]

2.   *It was narrated from 'Ali that a Jewish woman used to revile and disparage the Prophet. A man strangled her until she died, and the Messenger of Allah declared that no recompense was payable for her blood.*[91]

To further show that a prohibition against the killing of women and children was not a part of 7th century Islamic doctrine, take into consideration the following statement from the noted Islamic scholar al-Shafi'i, the founder of one of the major schools of Sharia Law:

> *...it is reported that Imam Ash-Shafi'i, may Allah have mercy upon him, said that he does not know anything that was prohibited then permitted and thereafter, prohibited once again except Nikah Mut'a.*[92]

As we have seen, the killing of women and children had been allowed, then prohibited, and then allowed again, with this cycle, and variations of

---

[90]   *Sunan Abu Dawud*, Vol. 5, No. 4361, pp. 20-21. This narration was also reported in *Sunan An-Nasa'i*, Vol. 5, No. 4075, pp. 66-67; in this particular *hadith* Muhammad said, "I bear witness that her blood is permissible."

[91]   *Sunan Abu Dawud*, Vol. 5, No. 4362, p. 21.

[92]   *In Defence of the True Faith*, p. 275. *Nikah Mut'a* was the "temporary marriage" that Muhammad had allowed his warriors to engage in when they were away from their wives on military campaigns.

54

it, being repeated a number of times. Al-Shafi'i stated that in terms of Islamic doctrine, the only thing that had been forbidden, then permitted, and then again finally forbidden, was *Nikah Mut'a*.

And al-Shafi'i should know:

> *In Koranic exegesis, he was the first to formulate the principles of the science of which verses abrogate others and which are abrogated...His knowledge of the Koran and sunna and of the accord between the different elements of each and the conditionality and explanation of some by others were* [sic] *incomparable.*[93]

So we see in this chapter that the prohibition against the killing of women and children was a specific, situational prohibition determined by Muhammad, instead of a general, all-encompassing command that was a part of Islamic doctrine.

The Islamic teachings about the killing of women and children were well summed up in a chapter of an essay titled *The Clarification Regarding Intentionally Targetting Women and Children*; here we learn when it is permissible to unintentionally kill women and children, and when it is permissible to intentionally kill them: [94]

---

[93]   Ahmad ibn Naqib al-Misri, *Reliance of the Traveller (Umdat al-Salik), A Classic Manual of Islamic Sacred Law*, edited and translated by Nuh Ha Mim Keller (Revised Edition 1994; rpt. Beltsville, Maryland: Amana Publications, 2008), x324, pp. 1095-1096.

[94]   "Situations When the General Prohibition is Restricted," *The Clarification Regarding Intentionally Targetting Women and Children*, pp. 24-39. It is difficult to see how the adjective "general" can be used when there are so many exceptions to the "General Prohibition" mentioned in this writing. This is another argument in favor of Muhammad's prohibition against the killing of women and children being specific and situational, instead of general.

Unintentionally Killing Women and Children

1. During a raid, day or night, when the Muslim warriors are unable to distinguish between the fighters and the women and children.

2. When the *kuffar* (non-Muslims) use their women and children as human shields, then it is permissible to kill them all. Shaykh Yusuf Al-'Uyayri made an important distinction here:

    > So if the human shields being used are Muslims, then the enemy should not be attacked except in the case of dire necessity...But if the kuffar use their own women and children as human shields, then this situation is not as grave as the first situation...It is permissible to kill those kuffar along with those (women and children) who are (originally) protected, if there is any need to do so – even if that need is not a dire necessity; because the protection placed upon the blood of the women and children of the kuffar is less than that of a Muslim (i.e. the blood of the Muslims is more valuable and protected)...[95]

3. When a catapult is used, it is permissible to attack the *kuffar*, even if it kills their women and children; this also applies to modern day weapons such as heavy artillery, planes and bombs.

4. When there is a need to besiege and burn fortresses and homes, and sink ships of the *kuffar*.

Intentionally Killing Women and Children

1. When the women and children of the *kuffar* fight against Muslims.

---

[95]   Ibid., p. 28.

2. When any of them encourages their fighters, or supports them, or distracts the Muslims. For example:

> *Ibn Qudamah Al-Maqdisi (ra) said, "If a woman stands in the ranks of the kuffar, or upon their fortress, and ridicules the Muslims, or reveals her naked self [as a distraction] – then <u>it is permissible to strike her.</u>* [sic] *As it is narrated on the authority of 'Ikrimah (ra), "When the Messenger besieged the People of At-Tā'if, a woman came up and revealed her naked body. So the Messenger ordered, "<u>Strike her!</u>* [sic]*" So a Muslim man struck her." And this was not a mistake from him. And it is permissible to look at her private parts- in such a situation- since it is necessary to look at the target. <u>And similarly, it is permissible to strike anyone who is (originally) protected from killing, such as a child or an old man and such</u>* [sic] *– if she (or they) prepares arrows for the enemy, gives them water to drink, or encourages them to fight; because they will be considered as fighters.*[96]

3. When they apostatize, then it is obligatory to kill all apostates, even if they are women.

4. When they curse the Prophet, or ridicule anything which manifests Islam. Manifestations of Islam are found, for example, in the *Ka'bah* in Mecca and the *Mus'haf* (the written/printed text of the Koran).

5. When they are the leaders of their people (e.g., queen, princess, prince).

---

[96]   Ibid., p. 31.

57

6. When the *kuffar* break their covenant, the Imam can choose to kill them all, including their women and children, or to save part of them.

7. When the *kuffar* target the women, children, and the elderly of the Muslims, then it is permissible to do the same thing to the women, children, and elderly of the *kuffar*.[97]

This chapter in the essay ended with an apt summary:

> *These are some of the situations which are exceptions to the general prohibition against killing women and children of the kuffar; amongst these situations, it is permissible to sometimes kill them intentionally, and also unintentionally – as long as there is a Maslahah [benefit (in this case, greater than the benefit of enslaving them)] for the Muslims and Mujahidin in doing so.*
>
> *So all these prove that the protection ['Ismah] of their blood is not unrestricted – unlike the prohibition of fornication and sodomy and the likes, which are unrestrictedly forbidden. Rather – the Shari'ah of Islam has made the blood of their women and children permissible in these exceptions. So this reveals the mistake of the people who claim that their protection ['Ismah] is unrestricted and absolute under all circumstances.[98]*

---

[97]   For more on this idea of equal retaliation, see Chapter 11, *The Law of Equality (Qisas)*.

[98]   *The Clarification Regarding Intentionally Targetting Women and Children*, p. 39.

5

Killing of Non-Combatants

It is important to note that the distinction between non-combatants and combatants is not found in the doctrines of Islam. Instead, the fundamental distinction is between Muslims (believers) and non-Muslims (disbelievers).

This distinction has been in place since the early days of Islam. According to the teachings of Muhammad, as long as a Muslim remained a Believer and did not violate any of the doctrines of Islam, he was not to be harmed by another Muslim:

> *Abu Huraira reported that Allah's Messenger (may peace be upon him) had said:...A Muslim is the brother of a Muslim. He neither oppresses him nor humiliates him nor looks down upon him...All things of a Muslim are inviolable for his brother in faith; his blood, his wealth and his honour.[99]*

This was also commanded by Allah in Chapter 4, Verses 92-93 of the Koran:

> *It is not for a believer to kill a believer except (that it be) by mistake...And whoever kills a believer intentionally, his recompense is Hell to abide therein; and the Wrath and the Curse of Allah are upon him, and a great punishment is prepared for him.*

---

[99] *Sahih Muslim*, Vol. 7, No. 2564, p. 173.

However, Muhammad said there were three conditions that allowed a Muslim to intentionally kill another Muslim:

> *It was narrated from 'Aishah that the Messenger of Allah said: "It is not permissible to shed the blood of a Muslim except in three cases: A adulterer who had been married, who should be stoned to death; a man who killed another man intentionally* [and without legal authority], *who should be killed; and a man who left Islam and waged war against Allah, the Mighty and Sublime, and His Messenger, who should be killed, or crucified, or banished from the land."*[100]

These teachings and commands about the inviolability of a brother Muslim were at the forefront of the minds of the *Al-Shabaab* attackers that day at the Westgate mall; the *Al-Shabaab* magazine noted:

> *Also safeguarding the inviolable blood of the Muslims, the Mujahideen separated the Muslims from the Kuffar* [disbelievers] *before beginning their attack.*[101]

However, with regard to non-Muslims, Muhammad taught that their "blood and property" were not protected from the Muslims unless they converted to Islam:

> *It has been narrated on the authority of 'Abdullah b. 'Umar that the Messenger of Allah said: I have been commanded to fight against people till they testify that there is no god but Allah, and Muhammad is the Messenger of Allah, they establish the prayer, and pay the Zakat. If they do it, their blood and property are*

---

[100] *Sunan An-Nasa'i*, Vol. 5, No. 4053, pp. 56-57.

[101] *Gaidi Mtaani*, p. 16.

*guaranteed protection on my behalf except when justified
by law, and their affairs rest with Allah.*[102]

That non-Muslims were to be fought against and were not protected unless
they converted to Islam is openly proclaimed by Allah in Chapter 9, Verse
5 of the Koran; this is the verse referred to by Muslim scholars as the
Verse of the Sword:

> *Then when the Sacred Months (the 1ˢᵗ, 7ᵗʰ, 11ᵗʰ, and 12ᵗʰ
> months of the Islamic calendar) have passed, then kill the
> Mushrikun wherever you find them, and capture them and
> besiege them, and lie in wait for them in every ambush.
> But if they repent [by rejecting Shirk (polytheism) and
> accept Islamic Monotheism] and perform As-Salat (the
> prayers), and give Zakat (obligatory charity), then leave
> their way free. Verily, Allah is Oft-Forgiving, Most
> Merciful.*

This command of Allah to *kill the Mushrikun* was followed during the time
of Muhammad as Muslim warriors attacked unsuspecting, non-Muslim
communities late at night or early in the morning to the undiscriminating
battle cries of *Kill! Kill!*[103] and *O victorious one, slay, slay!*.[104]

---

[102]   *Sahih Muslim*, Vol. 1, No. 22, pp. 21-22. There are similar *hadiths*
reporting that Muhammad said he had been commanded to fight until Islam was
made supreme, e.g.: *Sahih Al-Bukhari*, Vol. 1, Book 2, No. 25, p. 66; Vol. 4, Book
56, No. 2946, p. 126; *Jami' At-Tirmidhi*, Vol. 5, No. 2606, p. 15, and No. 2608,
pp. 17-18; Vol. 6, No. 3341, p. 76; *Sunan Ibn Majah*, Vol. 1, Nos. 71-72, pp. 123-
124; *Sunan An-Nasa'i*, Vol. 4, No. 3092, p. 18, and No. 3097, pp. 21-22; and
Sunan Abu Dawud, Vol. 3, No. 2641, p. 277.

[103]   E.g., *The History of al-Tabari: The Victory of Islam*, p. 142; *The Life of
Muhammad: Al-Waqidi's Kitab al-Maghazi*, p. 355; *Sunan Abu Dawud*, Vol. 3,
No. 2638, pp. 275-276; and *Kitab al-Tabaqat al-Kabir*, Vol. 2, p. 146.

[104]   E.g., *The Life of Muhammad*, n. 738, p. 768, and n. 760, p. 770; *The Life
of Muhammad: Al-Waqidi's Kitab al-Maghazi*, p. 549; and *Kitab al-Tabaqat al-
Kabir*, Vol. 2, p. 237.

Muhammad even stated that there was to be no penalty for a Muslim who killed a non-Muslim (disbeliever), with no distinction being made between a combatant and a non-combatant:

> *It was narrated from 'Amr bin Shu'aib, from his father, from his grandfather that the Messenger of Allah said: "A Muslim should not be killed in retaliation for the murder of a disbeliever."[105]*

And it is significant to note that Ibn Kathir, an authoritative 14th century Islamic scholar and commentator on the Koran, said this about that statement by Muhammad:

> *No opinion that opposes this ruling could stand correct, nor is there an authentic Hadith to contradict it.[106]*

During the time of Muhammad there were numerous incidents in which non-Muslims were killed by Muslims, whether they had surrendered after battle or were simply non-combatants.

---

[105]   *Sunan Ibn Majah*, Vol. 3, No. 2659, p. 528. This statement by Muhammad was also reported by Ibn 'Abbas, see *Sunan Ibn Majah*, Vol. 3, No. 2660, p. 529. The legal ruling that a Muslim was not to be killed for killing a non-Muslim was also reported by the fourth Caliph, Ali bin Abi Talib: e.g. *Sunan Ibn Majah*, Vol. 3, No. 2658, p. 528; and *Sahih Al-Bukhari*, Vol. 4, Book 56, No. 3047, p. 177.

[106]   *Tafsir Ibn Kathir*, Vol. 1, p. 485. The significance of Ibn Kathir's statement lies in the fact that his commentaries are still considered authoritative today. In the publisher's comments in 2000 for the ten volume English translation of Ibn Kathir's commentaries, it was pointed out that this collection

> *is the most popular interpretation of the Qur'an in the Arabic language, and the majority of the Muslims consider it to be the best source based on Qur'an and Sunnah.*

Tafsir Ibn Kathir, Vol. 1, p. 5.

For example, after the Muslims had emigrated from Mecca to Medina, the first major battle between the Muslims and their Meccan adversaries occurred in March 624 AD: the Battle of Badr. The Meccans were defeated. Among the Meccan captives were a man named Umayya bin Khalaf, and his son. As they were being led away, unarmed, and to be held for future ransom, some of the Muslims recognized Umayya and his son and they killed them both with swords. When Muhammad found out about these killings, he made no objection.[107]

As Muhammad gained power he personally ordered the killing of a number of non-Muslim poets and others who had criticized him and/or Islam (e.g. Ka'b b. al-Ashraf, Abu Rafi', 'Asma' bint Marwan, Abu 'Afak, and a singing girl named Quraybah).

Muhammad's attitude and actions were best summed up in a letter written shortly after the Muslim conquest of Mecca in 630 AD. It was sent to a non-Muslim poet who used to satirize Muhammad, from the poet's brother; here is a portion of that letter:

> *Allah's Messenger killed some men in Makkah who used*
> *to satirize and harm him, and the poets who survived fled*
> *in all directions for their lives. So, if you want to save*
> *your skin, hasten to Allah's Messenger. He never kills*
> *those who come to him repenting. If you refuse to do as I*
> *say, it is up to you to try to save your skin by any means.*[108]

So to save their lives from Muhammad, <u>poets</u> had to flee Mecca. This story had a happy ending, because after further correspondence between the brothers, the poet travelled to Medina, converted to Islam, and was forgiven by Muhammad.

---

[107] *Essay Regarding the Basic Rule of the Blood, Wealth and Honour of the Disbelievers*, p. 24.

[108] *The Sealed Nectar*, p. 521.

At one time Muhammad even gave a general order to kill any of the Jews that fell into a Muslim's hands:

> *The Messenger of God said, "Whoever of the Jews falls into your hands, kill him." So Muhayyisah b. Mas'ud [a* Muslim warrior] *fell upon Ibn Sunaynah, one of the Jewish merchants who was on close terms with them and used to trade with them, and killed him.*[109]

And there were examples of individual Muslims taking the initiative to kill non-Muslims for criticizing Muhammad and/or Islam – including, as mentioned in the previous chapter, the killing of two women! When Muhammad was told of these, he gave his approval.[110]

And after the defeat of the Jewish Bani Qurayzah tribe, Muhammad supervised the beheading of 600-900 captured males of the tribe. He ordered that <u>all</u> of the males who had reached puberty were to be killed; whether or not they were combatants was irrelevant.[111] Muhammad

---

[109] *The History of al-Tabari: The Foundation of the Community*, p. 97. This is also reported in *The Life of Muhammad*, p. 369; and *Sunan Abu Dawud*, Vol. 3, No. 3002, p. 499.

[110] **1)** A Muslim stabbed to death his pregnant female slave: *Sunan Abu Dawud*, Vol. 5, No. 4361, pp. 20-21; and *Sunan An-Nasa'i*, Vol. 5, No. 4075, pp. 66-67. **2)** A Muslim strangled a Jewish woman: *Sunan Abu Dawud*, Vol. 5, No. 4362, p. 21. **3)** A Muslim killed a man who said he did not believe in Islam and would never become a Muslim: *The History of al-Tabari: The Foundation of the Community*, pp. 149-150; this is also related in *The Life of Muhammad*, pp. 674-675.

[111] *The History of al-Tabari: The Victory of Islam*, p. 38; *The Life of Muhammad*, pp. 465-466; and *In Defence of the True Faith*, p. 206.

sent for them and struck off their heads...as they were
brought out to him in batches...This went on until the
apostle [Muhammad] *made an end of them.*[112]

Muhammad even specifically ordered that elderly non-Muslims were to be killed:

It was reported from Al-Hasan, from Samurah bin Jundab
who said: "The Messenger of Allah said: 'Kill the old
polytheist men, but spare their children.'"[113]

So we can see that Muhammad not only condoned the killing of non-combatant, non-Muslims, he even ordered it.

The Islamic doctrinal basis for this crucial distinction between Muslims and non-Muslims, and its ramifications, are well addressed in a piece titled *Essay Regarding the Basic Rule of the Blood, Wealth and Honour of the Disbelievers.* This essay points out that there are only six ways in which "the blood, wealth and honour of the disbelievers" is protected from Muslims:[114]

---

[112]   *The Life of Muhammad*, p. 464.

[113]   *Sunan Abu Dawud*, Vol. 3, No. 2670, p. 296. A variation of this, specifying pre-pubescent boys instead of children in general, was reported in *Jami' At-Tirmidhi*:

Samurah bin Jundab narrated that the Messenger of Allah said:
"Kill the elder men among the idolaters and spare the Sharkh
among them."

Jami' At-Tirmidhi, Vol. 3, No. 1583, p. 353. The commentary for this *hadith* noted that "the *Sharkh* are the boys who did not begin to grow public hair."

[114]   *Essay Regarding the Basic Rule of the Blood, Wealth and Honour of the Disbelievers*, pp. 10-17.

1. The Security (*Amān*) of *Thimmah* [*Dhimmah*] (tribute): This is a situation in which a non-Muslim living in a Muslim country pays the *Jizyah* (tribute, protection money).[115]

2. The Security of *Jawār* (seeking knowledge about Islām): Ibn Qudāmah explained,

    > *And whoever seeks security so that he can hear the words of Allāh and learn the legislations of Islām, then it is obligatory to give him that. Then he is returned to where he can be secure* [his home country].

3. The Security of *Sulh* (treaty): Muslims are allowed to enter into such a treaty only if:

    a. They are in a period of weakness vis-à-vis their enemy.
    b. They hope this will result in their enemy becoming Muslims.
    c. The enemy will pay the *Jizyah*.
    d. There is a general benefit to the Muslims.

    But such a treaty must have a specified time period because otherwise "this results in the complete abandonment of the *Jihād*."

---

[115]   This is specifically mentioned as a form of security for Jews and Christians in 9:29 of the Koran:

> *Fight against those who believe not in Allah, nor in the Last Day, nor forbid that which has been forbidden by Allah and His Messenger (Muhammad), and those who acknowledge not the religion of truth (i.e. Islam) among the people of the Scripture (Jews and Christians), until they pay the Jizyah with willing submission, and feel themselves subdued.*

However, throughout the history of the Muslim conquests there have been various Muslim rulers who allowed others to also pay the *Jizyah* as an alternative to death or conversion to Islam.

4. The Security of the Messengers: This allows information to be exchanged.

5. The Security of the Muslim in the Land of the Disbelievers: This is a two-way street in that the disbelievers promise not to harm the Muslim and the Muslim promises not to harm the disbelievers.

6. The Security of the Disbeliever in the Land of the Muslims: This is essentially the same as No. 5. There is an exception though if the non-Muslim enters Muslim lands governed by "apostate rulers who have allied themselves with the disbelievers or who rule with the fabricated laws of disbelief (Kufr)…" In that case, the security guaranteed by "apostate rulers" is not recognized by Muslims.

This essay succinctly points out that the existence of a security covenant on the part of a non-Muslim is the only condition that matters in terms of protecting that non-Muslim; hostility or lack of hostility toward Muslims is irrelevant:

> *The differences between those without a covenant (Amān) from the Muslims and those with one, is the difference between those whose blood and wealth is permitted and those whose blood is protected, as it has passed. And the one who does have a covenant of Amān from the Muslims is the Mu'āhad or Musta'man whereas the one without any covenant is the Muhārib or Harbī. And this label (i.e. Muhārib or Harbī) applies even if this disbeliever is not presently at war with the Muslims, because his label is based on the absence of a covenant, which protects his blood and wealth, and is not conditional upon his hostility towards the Muslims.*[116]

---

[116] *Essay Regarding the Basic Rule of the Blood, Wealth and Honour of the Disbelievers*, p. 17.

The essay was later more specific in terms of the rule applying beyond the battlefield:

> ...it is the characteristic of disbelief (Kufr) itself, which permits the blood and wealth of the disbelievers and not the battle. And although it is the battlefield where this rule is most often applied, this does not mean that applying it outside of the battlefield is prohibited.[117]

The essay also noted that the four major Sunni schools of Sharia Law were in agreement with this understanding about the treatment of non-Muslims:

> And we see when examining the discussions of the four Imāms and the students of their schools, that when they permitted killing and seizing the wealth of the disbelievers, they did so clearly based on the absence of any covenant ('Ahd) as well as the basic rule (Asl) that their blood and wealth were permissible do [sic] to their disbelief and not necessarily because of any hostility towards the Muslims.[118]

So for the non-Muslim who is not a combatant, the only sure way of not being killed by *jihadists* is to either convert to Islam or obtain a security covenant.

---

[117]   Ibid., p. 39.

[118]   Ibid., p. 24.

6

Mistreatment and Torture of Captives

The doctrines of Islam allow Muslims to mistreat, and even torture, their captives. We will start with the Koran, which provides the context for such treatment.

The Koran says that Muslims are the "best of creatures":

Chapter 98, Verse 7

> *Verily, those who believe [in the Oneness of Allah, and in His Messenger (Muhammad) including all obligations ordered by Islam] and do righteous good deeds, they are the best of creatures.*

This is reiterated in 3:110 where Muslims are proclaimed to be "the best of peoples ever raised up for mankind."

In contrast, Jews, Christians, and other non-Muslims are among "the worst of creatures":

Chapter 98, Verse 6

> *Verily, those who disbelieve (in the religion of Islam, the Qur'an and Prophet Muhammad) from among the people of the Scripture (Jews and Christians) and Al-Mushrikun, will abide in the fire of Hell. They are the worst of creatures.*

And 8:22 states that non-Muslims in general are "the worst of living creatures."

69

So what does the Koran say is to be done with those who are "the worst of living creatures"? Allah sets the example in these verses:

Chapter 3, Verse 56

> *"As to those who disbelieve, I* [Allah] *will punish them with a severe torment in this world and in the Hereafter, and they will have no helpers."*

Chapter 3, Verse 151

> *We* [Allah speaking in the third person] *shall cast terror into the hearts of those who disbelieve, because they joined others in worship with Allah, for which He had sent no authority; their abode will be the Fire and how evil is the abode of the Zalimun (polytheists and wrongdoers).*

This was reiterated in Chapter 8, Verse 12:

> *(Remember) when your Lord revealed to the angels, "Verily, I am with you, so keep firm those who have believed. I will cast terror into the hearts of those who have disbelieved...*

So how does Allah command the Muslims themselves to treat non-Muslims? The Muslims are to follow Allah's example. Let's look at a few relevant verses in the Koran:

Chapter 4, Verse 101

> *...verily, the disbelievers are ever to you open enemies.*

Chapter 9, Verse 14

> *Fight against them so that Allah will punish them by your hands and disgrace them and give you victory over them and heal the breasts of a believing people.*

> ****This was one of the Koran verses mentioned in the speech by *Al-Shabaab's* leader about the attack on the Westgate Mall.****

Chapter 9, Verse 73

> *O Prophet (Muhammad)! Strive hard against the disbelievers and the hypocrites, and be harsh against them, their abode is Hell, - and worst indeed is that destination.*

Chapter 9, Verse 123

> *O you who believe! Fight those of the disbelievers who are close to you, and let them find harshness in you; and know that Allah is with those who are Al-Muttaqun (the pious).*

Chapter 48, Verse 29

> *Muhammad is the Messenger of Allah. And those who are with him are severe against disbelievers, and merciful among themselves...*

Chapter 66, Verse 9

> *O Prophet (Muhammad)! Strive hard against the*
> *disbelievers and the hypocrites, and be severe against*
> *them; their abode will be Hell, - and worst indeed is that*
> *destination.*

And Muslims can even severely hurt non-Muslims as a warning, and in order to create fear among other non-Muslims. This is found in Chapter 8, Verse 57:

> *So if you gain the mastery over them in war, punish them*
> *severely in order to disperse those who are behind them,*
> *so that they may learn a lesson.*

Muhammad himself provided the example for such treatment of non-Muslims. He was proud that he had been made victorious with terror cast into the hearts of his enemies:

> *Narrated Abu Hurairah: Allah's Messenger said, "I have*
> *been sent with the shortest expressions bearing the widest*
> *meanings, and I have been made victorious with terror*
> *(cast in the hearts of the enemy), and while I was sleeping,*
> *the keys of the treasures of the world were brought to me*
> *and put in my hand."*[119]

He was also proud that fear of him had spread far and wide:

> *It was narrated that Jabir bin 'Abdullah said: "The*
> *Messenger of Allah said: 'I have been given five things*
> *that were not given to anyone before me: I have been*
> *supported with fear being struck into the hearts of my*
> *enemy for a distance of one month's travel...*[120]

---

[119]   *Sahih Al-Bukhari*, Vol. 4, Book 56, No. 2977, p. 140.

[120]   *Sunan An-Nasa'i*, Vol. 1, No. 432, p. 254.

And those who opposed him "were humiliated and made inferior":

> ...*Imam Ahmad narrated that Ibn 'Umar said that the Messenger of Allah said, I was sent with the sword just before the Last Hour, so that Allah is worshipped alone without partners. My sustenance was provided for me from under the shadow of my spear. Those who oppose my command were humiliated and made inferior, and whoever imitates a people, he is one of them.*[121]

> ****This was one of the *hadiths* mentioned in the statement by *Al-Shabaab's* leader about the attack on the Westgate Mall.****

There is at least one recorded incident in which Muhammad ordered the torture of two non-combatant, non-Muslims. When Kinanah bin al-Rabi of the Jewish Bani al-Nadir tribe would not reveal where his conquered tribe's treasures were hidden, Muhammad ordered one of his soldiers, "Torture him until you extract what he has," so a fire was built on Kinanah's chest until Kinanah nearly died. Kinanah's head was then cut off by one of the Muslims.[122] Muhammad then turned his attention to Kinanah's brother:

> *He commanded that the other Ibn Abi l-Huqayq (the brother of Kinana) also be tortured and then handed over to the care of Bishr b. al-Bara' to be killed by him. Some say that he cut off his head. After that the Messenger of*

---

[121]   *Tafsir Ibn Kathir*, Vol. 1, pp. 321-322. The phrase *under the shadow of my spear* refers to plunder obtained in battle.

[122]   *The Life of Muhammad*, p. 515. This was also related in *The History of al-Tabari: The Victory of Islam*, pp. 122-123. According to Al-Waqidi,

> *Al-Zubayr hurt him* [Kinanah]; *he came to him with a firebrand and pierced him in the chest.*

The Life of Muhammad: Al-Waqidi's Kitab al-Maghazi, p. 331.

God felt he had the right to their property and imprisoned their children.[123]

And then there was the case of Uqba bin Abu Mu'ayt. He had initially listened to Muhammad preaching in Mecca. However, after being soundly criticized for doing so, Uqba spat in Muhammad's face,[124] and then continued to mistreat Muhammad. [125] During the later Battle of Badr in March 624, Uqba was captured by the Muslims. After the battle was over, Muhammad ordered that Uqba be killed. Uqba said, "But who will look after my children, O Muhammad?" Muhammad replied, "Hell."[126] Muhammad then commanded,

"...Lead him, O 'Asim, and cut off his head." 'Asim did so.[127]

Then we have the previously mentioned example of cruelty to a captive that occurred during the Expedition to Wadi al-Qura in January of 628. This was the expedition led by Zayd bin Harithah, Muhammad's beloved, trusted, adopted son. Zayd commanded that an old woman from among the captives be killed, and she was tied to two camels and torn apart. There was no recorded comment from Muhammad about this cruel death.

So we can see that both the Koran and the teachings and example of Muhammad provide support for harsh, severe treatment, and even torture, of non-Muslim captives.

---

[123]   *The Life of Muhammad: Al-Waqidi's Kitab al-Maghazi*, p. 331.

[124]   *The Life of Muhammad*, p. 164.

[125]   Ibid., p. 191.

[126]   Ibid., p. 308.

[127]   *The Life of Muhammad: Al-Waqidi's Kitab al-Maghazi*, p. 57.

7

Raping Female Captives

But what about the raping of female captives? Unfortunately, support for this is also found in Islamic doctrine.

A female non-Muslim captive falls under the category of those "whom your right hands possess."[128] She then becomes a slave to her Muslim captor and it becomes "legal" for him to rape her. This is authorized by Chapter 4, Verse 24 of the Koran, which begins by stating

> *Also (forbidden are) women already married, except those (slaves) whom your right hands possess. Thus has Allah ordained for you...*

---

[128] The use of the phrase "whom your right hands possess" in reference to captured women and/or slave girls is found in both the Koran (e.g. 4:3, 4:24-25, 23:6, 24:31, 33:50, 33:52, and 70:30) and *hadiths* where it was used by Muhammad (e.g., *Sunan Ibn Majah*, Vol. 3, No. 1920, p. 101; *Sunan Abu Dawud*, Vol. 4, No. 4017, p. 381; *Jami' At-Tirmidhi*, Vol. 5, No. 2769, p. 141; and *Musnad Imam Ahmad Bin Hanbal*, Vol. 1, No. 736, p. 377).

Muhammad's favorite wife Aisha said that when it came to taking pledges from women, Muhammad's hand

> *did not touch any woman's hand except the hand of the woman that his right hand possessed (i.e. his captives or his lady-slaves).*

Sahih Al-Bukhari, Vol. 9, Book 93, No. 7214, p. 203.

The phrase was also used by some Muslims in general (e.g., *Sahih Al-Bukhari*, Vol. 7, Book 67, No. 5159, p. 69; and *Sunan An-Nasa'i*, Vol. 4, No. 3384, p. 185).

Ibn Kathir, our authoritative Islamic scholar, explained the meaning of this verse:

> The Ayah [verse] *means, you are prohibited from marrying women who are already married, (except those whom your right hands possess) except those whom you acquire through war, for you are allowed such women after making sure they are not pregnant. Imam Ahmad recorded that Abu Sa'id Al-Khudri said, "We captured some women from the area of Awtas who were already married, and we disliked having sexual relations with them because they already had husbands. **So, we asked the Prophet about this matter, and this Ayah was revealed...Consequently we had sexual relations with these women.*[129]* [my emphasis]

---

[129]   *Tafsir Ibn Kathir*, Vol. 2, p. 422. The raid on Awtas occurred in January 630. This question regarding what to do with the captured women, with the same conclusion, was also reported in *Sunan Abu Dawud*, Vol. 2, No. 2155, pp. 555-556; *Jami' At-Tirmidhi*, Vol. 2, No. 1132, pp. 502-503; and Vol. 5, Nos. 3016-3017, pp. 331-332; *Sunan An-Nasa'i*, Vol. 4, No. 3335, p. 155; and Abu'l-Hasan 'Ali ibn Ahmad ibn Muhammad ibn 'Ali al-Wahidi, *Al-Wahidi's Asbab al-Nuzul*, trans. Mokrane Guezzou (Louisville, KY: Fons Vitae, 2008), p. 71.

A modern commentary pointed out that this became a *permanent principle*:

> For a solution and as a permanent principle regarding war captives, particularly those who are given a female captive as their share from the spoils of war, even though her non-believer and polytheist husband is alive; the recipient was allowed to have sexual intercourse with her after finding out the condition of her womb...

Jami' At-Tirmidhi, Vol. 5, Comment to *Hadith* No. 3016, p. 331.

The modern *Tafsir Ahsanul-Bayan*, explained 4:24 this way:

> *The historical background of the verse is that when pagan*
> *women were captured by Muslims in battles, they disliked*
> *having intercourse with them because they had husbands.*
> *The Companions asked the Messenger of Allah about it.*
> *Thereupon, this verse was revealed. The verse allowed*
> *the Muslims to have intercourse with pagan women if they*
> *were captured in battles even if they had husbands,*
> *providing their wombs have been cleansed, that is, after*
> *one menses or, in case they are pregnant, after the*
> *delivery of the child.*[130]

So when his warriors asked him about raping female captives, instead of prohibiting it, Muhammad responded with this approving "revelation" from Allah.

And Muhammad was actively involved in allowing the rape of female captives. After the defeat of the Jewish Bani Qurayzah tribe, Muhammad divided up that tribe's "property, wives, and children" among the Muslims.[131] And after the defeat of the Jews at Khaybar, Muhammad had the women of Khaybar "distributed among the Muslims."[132]

But what does Islamic sacred law have to say about this? It should not be surprising to note that the founders of the four major Sunni schools of Sharia Law agreed with this:

> *This issue is agreed upon by all Four A'immah* [Scholars];
> *when a married woman becomes a prisoner of war*

---

[130]   Salahuddin Yusuf, *Tafsir Ahsanul-Bayan*, trans. Mohammad Kamal Myshkat, Vol. 1 (Riyadh, Kingdom of Saudi Arabia: Darussalam, 2010), pp. 441-442.

[131]   *The Life of Muhammad*, p. 466.

[132]   Ibid., p. 511.

*without her husband, her contract of marriage with her
husband ends, and her new master has the right to have
sexual relations with her after the birth of a child if she is
pregnant, or after waiting a while to confirm the status of
her womb if she is not apparently pregnant.* [133]

And according to the Koran (33:50), although a Muslim was limited to
only four wives, there were no limitations on the number of slave girls he
could possess. [134]

An interesting distinction was made by Ibn Salih Al-Uthaymin, a 20th
century Muslim scholar:

*Then if someone says: 'If they rape our women then do we
rape their woman?' No, this, no, no we do not do it.
Why? Because this is prohibited as a (whole)
category...Meaning, it is **not** [sic] forbidden out of respect
for the rights of others [i.e. not because we are respecting
their rights] – **rather** [sic], because it is forbidden as a
category...But if the dividing (of the Ghanimah) [spoils of
war] takes place, and the woman from them ends up as a
slave woman, then she becomes property of the right*

---

[133]   *Jami' At-Tirmidhi*, Vol. 2, Comment to *Hadith* No. 1132, p. 503.

[134]   From the commentaries on 33:50: *Tafsir Ibn Kathir*, Vol. 7, p. 724;
Tafsir Ahsanul-Bayan, Vol. 4, p. 402; *Tafsir Ibn 'Abbas*, trans. Mokrane Guezzou
(Louisville, KY: Fons Vitae, 2008), p. 551; and Jalalu'd-Din Al-Mahalli and
Jalalu'd-Din As-Suyuti, *Tafsir Al-Jalalayn*, trans. Aisha Bewley (London: Dar Al
Taqwa Ltd., 2007), p. 907.

The lack of limits on the number of slave girls is also noted in the Hanafi School
of Sharia Law, which states that "one may collect as many slave women as one
wishes," without "reckoning the number even if it exceeds a thousand." See Abu
Hanifah Nu'man ibn Thabit ibn Nu'man ibn al-Marzuban ibn Zuta ibn Mah, *The
Kitab al-Athar of Imam Abu Hanifah: The Narration of Imam Muhammad Ibn Al-
Hasan Ash-Shaybani*, trans. 'Abdassamad Clarke (London: Turath Publishing,
2007), 134.457 and n. 1347, p. 263.

hand. The person can have intercourse with her as a right hand possession, which is permissible and there is nothing wrong with this.[135]

So technically speaking, a non-Muslim female is not allowed to be raped until she and the rest of the plunder have been allocated among the Muslim warriors. And over the days in which the Westgate Mall was held by the *Mujahidin*, there was plenty of time to allocate the plunder.[136]

---

[135]   *The Clarification Regarding Intentionally Targetting Women and Children*, p. 73.

[136]   For a more detailed look at the phrase "whom your right hands possess," see Chapter 11, "Whom Your Right Hands Possess," in Stephen M. Kirby, *Letting Islam Be Islam: Separating Truth From Myth* (Charleston, South Carolina: CreateSpace, 2012).

8

Beheading

The beheading of non-Muslims is supported in the Koran. There are two verses that specifically deal with beheadings:

Chapter 8, Verse 12

> *(Remember) when your Lord revealed to the angels,*
> *"Verily, I am with you, so keep firm those who have*
> *believed. I will cast terror into the hearts of those who*
> *have disbelieved, so strike them over the necks, and smite*
> *over all their fingers and toes."*

This verse pertained to the Battle of Badr, in which the Muslims believed they had been assisted by angels. Ibn Kathir explained that in this verse Allah commanded the angels to do the following to the enemy:

> *...strike them on their foreheads to tear them apart and*
> *over the necks to cut them off, and cut off their limbs,*
> *hands and feet.* [137]

The *Tafsir Al-Jalalayn* explained that "strike their necks" meant to "behead them." [138]

One might claim that this verse states what Allah had commanded only the angels to do when they reportedly helped the Muslims during the Battle of

---

[137]   *Tafsir Ibn Kathir*, Vol. 4, p. 274.

[138]   *Tafsir Al-Jalalayn*, p. 379.

Badr. Consequently, the command to behead the enemy would not be applicable for the Muslims themselves. However, Ibn Jarir, an authoritative Islamic scholar, stated that the command to the angels in this verse to *smite over all their fingers and toes* was actually also a command to the Muslims to do the same to their enemies. [139] Therefore, it would be implied that Allah's command to the angels to *strike them over the necks* would then also be a command to the Muslims to do the same.

Nevertheless, Allah's command about beheading was later repeated directly to the Muslims in terms of how to deal with non-Muslims:

Chapter 47, Verse 4

> *So, when you meet (in fight – Jihad in Allah's Cause)*
> *those who disbelieve, smite (their) necks till when you*
> *have killed and wounded many of them, then bind a bond*
> *firmly (on them, i.e. take them as captives)...*

Muhammad also approved of beheadings and ordered many to be done:

1. On one occasion, Muhammad sent one of his warriors to behead a Muslim (*strike his neck*) who had illegally married a woman.[140]

2. On another occasion, Muhammad sent Ali to behead a man (*strike his neck*) who reportedly had illegal sexual intercourse with one of Muhammad's female slaves.[141]

---

[139] *Tafsir Ibn Kathir*, Vol. 4, p. 274.

[140] *Sunan Ibn Majah*, Vol. 3, No. 2608, pp. 494-495; also see No. 2607, p. 494 (*strike his neck*). Similar narrations were reported in *Sunan Abu Dawud*, Vol. 5, Nos. 4456-4457, pp. 75-76 (*struck his neck/strike his neck*). The woman was the wife of the Muslim's deceased father. Such a woman was considered *Mahram*, an unmarriageable relative, and such a marriage is strictly prohibited in 4:22 of the Koran.

[141] *Sahih Muslim*, Vol. 8, No. 2771, p. 281.

3. As was previously mentioned, after the Battle of Badr in March 624, Muhammad ordered the beheading of Uqba bin Abu Mu'ayt, a non-Muslim who had been captured during the battle.

4. Around September of 624, Muhammad wanted to kill Ka'b bin Al-Ashraf, a Jewish poet in Medina who had criticized him and written poetry offensive to Muslim women. Muhammad sent a small group of Muslims who tricked Ka'b into coming out of his house. They killed him, cut off his head, and gave it to Muhammad; Muhammad "praised Allah on his being slain."[142]

5. Around April of 627, after the defeat of the Jewish Bani Qurayzah tribe, Muhammad supervised the beheading of 600-900 males of the tribe, non-combatants included. He also ordered the beheading of one woman.

6. In May of 627, Muhammad sent a Muslim warrior, 'Abdullah b. Unays, to kill Sufyan b. Khalid. 'Abdullah befriended Sufyan, joined him in his tent, killed him, and then cut off his head. 'Abdullah brought Sufyan's head back to Muhammad, and Muhammad praised 'Abdullah.[143]

7. Around June 628, Muhammad ordered the torturing of Kinanah bin al-Rabi and his brother, both of the Jewish Bani al-Nadir tribe; after the torture, both were beheaded.

8. In November 629, a large group of the Jusham tribe, under the command of Rifa'ah b. Qays, had camped at al-Ghabah. Muhammad sent three Muslims to gather information or to bring back Rifa'ah. They killed Rifa'ah and beheaded him. The three

---

[142] *Kitab al-Tabaqat al-Kabir*, Vol. 2, p. 37. It was similarly reported in *The Life of Muhammad: Al-Waqidi's Kitab al-Maghazi*, p. 95; and *The Sealed Nectar*, p. 289.

[143] *The Life of Muhammad: Al-Waqidi's Kitab al-Maghazi*, p. 262. This was also reported in *Kitab al-Tabaqat al-Kabir*, Vol. 2, pp. 60-61.

Muslims then returned to Medina and presented Rifa'ah's head to Muhammad. Muhammad rewarded the leader with thirteen camels.[144]

9. From April 624 until January 630, Muhammad had a standing order to behead a certain non-Muslim if he was captured:

> *I have not seen the Messenger of God send an expedition ever, except he said: If you defeat Habbar cut off his hands and legs and then his head.*[145]

10. Muhammad specifically said, "If someone changes his religion - then strike off his head!"[146]

11. And Muhammad even said it was permissible to behead a person who denied a verse of the Koran:

> *It was narrated from Ibn 'Abbas that the Messenger of Allah said: "Whoever denies a Verse of the Qur'an, it is permissible to strike his neck..."*[147]

So support for beheading, even of non-combatants and captives, is found in the Koran and in the teachings and example of Muhammad.[148]

---

[144]   *The Life of Muhammad*, pp. 671-672.

[145]   *The Life of Muhammad: Al-Waqidi's Kitab al-Maghazi*, p. 422.

[146]   *Al-Muwatta of Imam Malik ibn Anas*, 36.18.15.

[147]   *Sunan Ibn Majah*, Vol. 3, No. 2539, p. 455.

[148]   In Rome on May 12, 2013, Pope Francis canonized 800 Italian men who had been beheaded by Muslims outside the Italian town of Otranto in 1480; their crime was refusing to convert to Islam after surrendering to the superior Muslim army. As we can see from this section, the Muslims were simply following the commands found in the Koran and the teachings and example of Muhammad when they beheaded the 800 Christian captives.

9

Mutilation

Support for mutilation can be found in Islamic doctrine. A verse of the Koran not only authorizes beheadings, but also commands cutting off the fingers and toes of those who do not believe in Islam:

Chapter 8, Verse 12

> *(Remember) when your Lord revealed to the angels,*
> *"Verily, I am with you, so keep firm those who have*
> *believed. I will cast terror into the hearts of those who*
> *have disbelieved, so strike them over the necks, and smite*
> *over all their fingers and toes."*

Although this verse states what Allah had commanded the angels to do when they reportedly helped the Muslims during the Battle of Badr, it was also a command for what the Muslims (believers) were to do to their enemies:

> *Ibn Jarir commented that this Ayah [verse] commands, "O*
> *believers! Strike every limb and finger on the hands and*
> *feet of your (disbelieving) enemies."[149]*

Why cut off fingers and toes? In the commentary about this verse of the Koran, the modern *Tafsir Ahsanul-Bayan* explained:

> *If the fingers of the hands are cut off, they will become*
> *unable to move their swords. Similarly, when the toes are*
> *cut off, they will be unable to run away.[150]*

---

[149]   *Tafsir Ibn Kathir*, Vol. 4, p. 274.

[150]   *Tafsir Ahsanul-Bayan*, Vol. 2, Commentary No. 2, p. 276.

In another verse we find that the "recompense" for those who wage war against Islam includes the amputation of hands and feet:

Chapter 5, Verse 33

> *The recompense of those who wage war against Allah and*
> *His Messenger and do mischief in the land is only that*
> *they shall be killed or crucified or their hands and their*
> *feet be cut off from opposite sides, or be exiled from the*
> *land. That is their disgrace in this world, and a great*
> *torment is theirs in the Hereafter.*

In case you are thinking that the phrase *those who wage war against Allah and His Messenger* pertains only to combatants, we need to consult one of our authoritative Islamic scholars. According to Ibn Kathir, to *wage war* against Allah and Muhammad meant to

> *oppose and contradict, and it includes disbelief, blocking*
> *roads and spreading fear in the fairways.*[151]

And what about *do mischief in the land*? Ibn Kathir agreed with a number of Muslim scholars, who said,

> *"Do not make mischief on the earth," means, "Do not*
> *commit acts of disobedience on the earth. Their mischief*
> *is disobeying Allah, because whoever disobeys Allah on*
> *the earth, or commands that Allah be disobeyed, he has*
> *committed mischief on the earth."*[152]

The authoritative *Tafsir Al-Jalalayn* used the word *corruption* instead of *mischief,* and *corruption* was defined as including *unbelief,*[153] which means not being a Muslim.

---

[151]   *Tafsir Ibn Kathir*, Vol. 3, p. 161.

[152]   Ibid., Vol. 1, pp. 131-132.

[153]   *Tafsir Al-Jalalayn*, p. 248.

So simply disobeying or not believing in Allah is to *wage war* against Islam and commit *mischief in the land*. Consequently, any non-Muslim is, by definition, committing these acts and could justifiably be killed or mutilated.

What did Muhammad have to say about mutilations? Initially he appeared not to have addressed it, and there was a recorded incident of what appeared to be the mutilation of the body of a dead Meccan after the Battle of Badr. As was previously mentioned, among the Meccan captives after that battle were a man named Umayya (Umaiyya) bin Khalaf, and his son. As they were being led away for future ransom by Abdu'l-Rahman, a Muslim warrior, others of the Muslims recognized them and set upon them. As Abdu'l-Rahman later explained it:

> *They hewed them to pieces with their swords until they were dead.*[154]

There are two authoritative *hadiths* indicating that Umayya's body appeared to have been mutilated after he was killed:

1. *Narrated 'Abdullah:...I saw these people killed on the day of (the battle of) Badr and thrown in the well, except Umaiyya or Ubai whose body parts were mutilated but he was not thrown in the well.*[155]

2. *It has been narrated by 'Abdullah...I saw that all were slain in the Battle of Badr and their dead bodies were thrown into a well, except that of Umayya or Ubayy, which was cut into pieces and was thrown into the well.*[156]

---

[154]   *The Life of Muhammad*, p. 303. For a similar narration in which Umayya and his son were "hacked" with swords "until they had finished with them," see *The History of al-Tabari: The Foundation of the Community*, p. 60.

[155]   *Sahih Al-Bukhari*, Vol. 5, Book 63, No. 3854, pp. 114-115.

[156]   *Sahih Muslim*, Vol. 6, No. 1794R1, p. 213.

However, there were other reports that when the time came to throw Umayya's body into the well with the other dead Meccans, his body had swollen up inside his suit of armor, or he was very fat, and he began to fall apart when the Muslims tried to move him; consequently, they left Umayya where he was and covered him with earth and stones.[157] In these particular reports there was no mention about Umayya's body being mutilated.

Nevertheless, at some point Muhammad issued orders in a context that prohibited the mutilation of dead bodies. For example, before he sent Muslim forces against non-Muslims, it was reported that he would issue the following order to the leader of those forces:

> ... Fight in the name of Allah and in the way of Allah. Fight against those who disbelieve in Allah. Make a holy war...do not mutilate (the dead) bodies...[158]

And on another occasion:

> Narrated 'Abdullah bin Yazid Al-Ansari: The Prophet forbade robbery (taking away what belongs to others by force without their permission), and also forbade the mutilation (or maiming) of bodies.[159]

---

[157]   The Life of Muhammad, p. 305; The History of al-Tabari: The Foundation of the Community, p. 62; and Sahih Al-Bukhari, Vol. 4, Book 58, No. 3185, p. 261.

[158]   Sahih Muslim, Vol. 5, No. 1731R1, p. 163. A second version of this hadith reported that Muhammad said, "...do not mutilate (the dead enemy)..."; see Sunan Abu Dawud, Vol. 3, No. 2613, p. 264. And in another version of this hadith Muhammad simply said, "...do not be treacherous, nor mutilate..."; see Jami' At-Tirmidhi, Vol. 3, No. 1408 p. 193.

[159]   Sahih Al-Bukhari, Vol. 3, Book 46, No. 2474, p. 380.

This understanding that mutilation applied to dead bodies was reiterated by Ibn Hajar, a noted 15th century Islamic scholar, when he explained the meaning of mutilation:

> *Mutilation means disfigurement of the appearance of a corpse; for example, chopping off limbs for it to be remembered (by the opposition), and the likes.[160]*

It should be noted that in *Sunan An-Nasa'i* we find a *hadith* stating simply that

> *...The Messenger of Allah used to stress charity in his sermons, and prohibit mutilation.[161]*

But the modern commentary for this *hadith* explained:

> *Mutilation means cutting or tearing off the limbs of the person slain (ear, nose, private parts, etc.) so that the corpse is debased or desecrated.[162]*

So Muhammad's command against mutilation was directed toward how dead bodies were to be treated.

But when it came to the living, here is a stark example of Muhammad ordering the mutilation and slow death of some captives in February 628:

---

[160]   *The Clarification Regarding Intentionally Targetting Women and Children*, p. 52.

[161]   *Sunan An-Nasa'i*, Vol. 5, No. 4052, p. 56.

[162]   Ibid. The understanding that the term *mutilation* pertained to actions done to dead bodies is also found in: *Sunan Ibn Majah*, Vol. 4, Comment to *Hadith* No. 3185, p. 286; and *Sunan Abu Dawud*, Vol. 3, Comment to *Hadith* No. 2667, p. 295. It is interesting to note that these comments in *Sunan Abu Dawud* also pointed out that *mutilation* included *mutilating the face while he lives*.

*Narrated Abu Qilaba: Anas said, "Some people of 'Uki or
'Uraina tribe came to Al-Madina and its climate did not
suit them. So the Prophet ordered them to go to the herd
of (milch) camels and to drink their milk and urine (as a
medicine). So they went as directed and after they became
healthy, they killed the shepherd of the Prophet and drove
away all the camels. The news reached the Prophet early
in the morning and he sent (men) in their pursuit and they
were captured and brought at noon. He then ordered to
cut* [off] *their hands and feet (and it was done), and their
eyes were branded with heated pieces of iron. They were
put in Al-Harra* [a place of stony ground in Medina] *and
when they asked for water, no water was given them."
Abu Qilaba added, "Those people committed theft,
murder, became disbelievers after embracing Islam
(Murtadin) and fought against Allah and His
Messenger.*"[163]

A modern commentary about this incident explained that this was a
justifiable punishment:

---

[163]   *Sahih Al-Bukhari*, Vol. 1, Book 4, No. 233, pp. 178-179. A similar
narration is found in *Sahih Al-Bukhari*, Vol. 4, Book 56, No. 3018, pp. 160-161;
and Vol. 7, Book 76, No. 5727, pp. 344-345; *Sahih Muslim*, Vol. 5, Nos. 1671-
1671R7, pp. 112-114; *Jami' At-Tirmidhi*, Vol. 1, Nos. 72-73, pp. 98-100; *Sunan
Ibn Majah*, Vol. 3, Nos. 2578-2579, p. 479; *Sunan An-Nasa'i*, Vol. 1, Nos. 306-
307, pp. 188-189; *Sunan Abu Dawud*, Vol. 5, Nos. 4364-4370, pp. 22-26; *Al-
Wahidi's Asbab al-Nuzul*, p. 93; and *The Life of Muhammad*, pp. 677-678.

In another *hadith* Anas reported something else he saw that day at *Al-Harra*:

I saw one of them licking the earth with his tongue till he died.

See *Sahih Al-Bukhari*, Vol. 7, Book 76, No. 5685, p. 328. Anas also reported that
he saw one of them "biting at the ground out of thirst, until they died." See *Sunan
Abu Dawud*, Vol. 5, No. 4367, p. 24.

89

Branding their eyes blind with heated iron instruments,
chopping off their hands and feet, abandoning them upon
burning rocks, not giving them any water despite their
being extremely thirsty, and their dying while writhing
around in agony – all of this was by way of just retribution
(Al-Qisas). For they had treated the Prophet's herdsman
in the same cruel manner. Hence, they were justifiably
punished.[164]

However, Allah "rebuked" Muhammad for the extent of these punishments and "revealed" a verse of the Koran that restricted, to a certain extent, the nature of such punishment:

It was narrated from Abu Az-Zinnad, that when the
Messenger of Allah cut off (the hands and feet) of those
who stole his camels and gouged out their eyes with fire,
Allah rebuked him for that and Allah revealed (the
words): The recompense of those who wage war against
Allah and His Messenger and do mischief in the land is
only that they shall be killed or crucified or their hands
and their feet be cut off from opposite sides, or be exiled
from the land. That is their disgrace in this world, and a
great torment is theirs in the Hereafter.[165]

So instead of gouging out the eyes and cutting off both of the hands and feet of an individual, punishment of that nature was now to be limited to only cutting off one hand and one foot, from opposite sides. This "revelation" from Allah was codified in 5:33 of the Koran.

And for many years Muhammad had a standing order for the live mutilation, and then killing of a particular non-Muslim:

---

[164]   *Sunan An-Nasa'i*, Vol. 1, Comment to *Hadith* No. 306, p. 188. For information about *Al-Qisas*, see Chapter 11, *The Law of Equality (Qisas)*.

[165]   *Sunan Abu Dawud*, Vol. 5, No. 4370, p. 26.

90

*As for Habbar b. al-Aswad, indeed the Messenger of God,
whenever he sent out an expedition, commanded it
regarding Habbar that if he were found he should be
burned in the fire. Then he changed his mind saying:
Surely only, the lord of the hell fire should cause such
suffering. Cut off his hands and his legs if you have power
over him, then kill him...His crime was that he sought out
the daughter of the Messenger of God, Zaynab, and struck
her back with a spear until she who was pregnant fell and
lost her baby. The Prophet permitted his blood.*[166]

This incident involving Zaynab occurred around April of 624, shortly after
the Battle of Badr. However, after the conquest of Mecca in January 630,
Habbar converted to Islam and was spared by Muhammad. This means
that for almost 6 years the Muslims had a standing order from Muhammad
that if they captured Habbar, before they killed him they were to mutilate
him by cutting off his hands and his legs.

The mutilation of living people was continued by Abu Bakr, who, after
Muhammad died, became the first of the four "Rightly Guided" Caliphs;
these first four caliphs were so named because they are believed to have
held the most firmly to the teachings of Muhammad. Abu Bakr started
holding fast to some of those teachings soon after Muhammad died:

*It is reported that certain women at an-Nujair having
rejoiced at the death of the Prophet, abu-Bakr wrote
ordering that their hands and feet be cut off. Among these
women were ath-Thabja' al-Hadramiyah, and Hind,
daughter of Yamin, the Jewess.*[167]

And also soon after Muhammad's death, two singing women appeared
before Al-Muhajir, the Muslim governor of the Yemen. One of them sang

---

[166]   *The Life of Muhammad: Al-Waqidi's Kitab al-Maghazi*, p. 422.

[167]   *The Origins of the Islamic State*, p. 155.

91

a song reviling Muhammad, and Al-Muhajir had her hand cut off and a front tooth pulled out. Caliph Abu Bakr wrote to Al-Muhajir:

> *I have learned what you did regarding the woman who sang and piped with abuse of the Apostle of God. If you had not beaten me to (punishing her), I would have ordered you to kill her, for the punishment (for abuse) of prophets is not like (other) punishments. So whoever does (something like) that among those claiming to be Muslims is (actually) an apostate; or among those claiming to be at peace with the Muslims is (actually) at war (with them) and a traitor...Now then: I have learned that you cut off the hand of a woman because she sang satirizing the Muslims, and that you pulled her front tooth. If she was among those who claim (to have embraced) Islam, then (it is) good discipline and a reprimand, and not mutilation.*[168]

So we can see that commands of the Koran, the teachings and example of Muhammad, and the subsequent actions of the first "Rightly Guided" Caliph, provide support for the idea that it is permissible for Muslims to mutilate those who are still alive.

---

[168]   Abu Ja'far Muhammad b. Jarir al-Tabari, *The History of al-Tabari: The Conquest of Arabia*, Vol. X, trans. and annotated Fred M. Donner (Albany, New York: State University of New York Press, 1993), pp. 191-192.

10

Burning the Folks

It is not unusual to hear that Islam prohibits burning people to death
because that is a punishment reserved only for Allah. Here is the *hadith*
used to support this claim:

> *Narrated Abu Hurairah: Allah's Messenger sent us in an*
> *expedition (i.e., an army-unit) and said, "If you find so-*
> *and-so and so-and-so, burn both of them with fire." When*
> *we intended to depart, Allah's Messenger said, "I have*
> *ordered you to burn so-and-so and so-and-so, and it is*
> *none but Allah Who punishes with fire, so, if you find*
> *them, kill them."*[169]

And there is a similar story about a specific individual:

> *As for Habbar b. al-Aswad, indeed the Messenger of God,*
> *whenever he sent out an expedition, commanded it*
> *regarding Habbar that if he were found he should be*
> *burned in the fire. Then he changed his mind saying:*
> *Surely only, the lord of the hell fire should cause such*
> *suffering. Cut off his hands and his legs if you have power*
> *over him, then kill him...*[170]

---

[169]   *Sahih Al-Bukhari*, Vol. 4, Book 56, No. 3016, p. 159. This *hadith* was
also reported in *Jami' At-Tirmidhi*, Vol. 3, No. 1572, p. 343.

[170]   *The Life of Muhammad: Al-Waqidi's Kitab al-Maghazi*, p. 422.

However, there are specific incidents in which Muhammad actually ordered the burning down of occupied structures. In December 627:

> *The Prophet launched a raid against the tribe of al-Mustalaq and they fought back. So he commanded to set fire to their fortifications all night long with the widespread knowledge that women and children were in there.*[171]

Around June 628, when Kinanah bin al-Rabi of the Jewish Bani al-Nadir tribe would not reveal where his conquered tribe's treasures were hidden, Muhammad ordered one of his soldiers, "Torture him until you extract what he has," so a fire was built on Kinanah's chest until Kinanah nearly died.[172]

In October 630 there was some resistance among the Muslims toward a military expedition Muhammad was planning against the Byzantines at Tabuk. Muhammad

> *heard that the hypocrites were assembling in the house of Suwaylim the Jew (his house was by Jasum) keeping men back from the apostle in the raid on Tabuk. So the prophet sent Talha b. 'Ubaydullah with a number of his friends to them with orders to burn Suwaylim's house down on them. Talha did so, and al-Dahhak b. Khalifa threw himself from the top of the house and broke his leg, and his friends rushed out and escaped.*[173]

In June 632, after Muhammad's death, the attack on Ubna that he had earlier ordered took place. The leader of the Muslim force said,

---

[171]   *The Al Qaeda Reader*, p. 167.

[172]   *The Life of Muhammad*, p. 515.

[173]   Ibid., n. 858, p. 782.

> *... the Messenger of God commanded me and this was his
> last command to me: To hasten the march...And to raid
> them, without inviting them* [to Islam], *and to destroy and
> burn.*[174]

And Muhammad even considered burning down Muslims' houses around
them to compel their attendance at congregational prayers:

> *It was narrated that Abu Hurairah said: "The Messenger
> of Allah said: 'I was thinking of commanding that the call
> to prayer be given, then I would tell a man to lead the
> people in prayer, then I would go out with some other men
> carrying bundles of wood, and go to people who do not
> attend the prayer, and burn their houses down around
> them.'"*[175]

So Muhammad's statements and actions show that during his lifetime it
was permissible to burn people, even Muslims, alive. This was continued
after Muhammad's death.

After Muhammad died there were many Arab tribes that left Islam. This
resulted in the Wars of Apostasy (*Riddah* Wars) under Abu Bakr, the first
"Rightly Guided" Caliph. Abu Bakr sent Muslim armies not only against

---

[174]   *The Life of Muhammad: Al-Waqidi's Kitab al-Maghazi*, p. 549.

[175]   *Sunan Ibn Majah*, Vol. 1, No. 791, pp. 513-514. Similar *hadiths* were
reported in *Sunan Ibn Majah*, Vol. 1, No. 795, pp. 515-516 (*I will burn their
houses down*); *Sahih Al-Bukhari*, Vol. 1, Book No. 10, No. 644, pp. 371-372
(*burn the houses of men who did not present themselves*); No. 657, p. 376 (*to burn
all those men (along with their houses)*); *Sahih Muslim*, Vol. 2, No. 651R2 (*burn
the houses with their inmates (who have not joined the congregation)*), and No.
652 (*burn those men who do not attain the Friday prayer in their houses*), p. 367;
Sunan An-Nasa'i, Vol. 1, No. 849, p. 502 (*to those men and burned their houses
down over them*); *Sunan Abu Dawud*, Vol. 1, No. 549, p. 340 (*go to (the houses)
of people who pray in their houses while having no excuse (to stay away from the
Masjid* [mosque]*), so that I may burn it down*); and *Al-Muwatta of Imam Malik
ibn Anas*, 8.1.3 (*burn their houses down about them*).

95

the apostate tribes, but also against Arab tribes that had not been previously conquered during the time of Muhammad. The commander of each army had a letter from Abu Bakr to be read to the people before any non-Muslim tribe was attacked. The letter explained:

> *I have sent to you someone at the head of an army of the Muhajirun and the Ansar and those who follow [them] in good works. I ordered him not to fight anyone or to kill anyone until he has called him to the cause of God; so that those who respond to him and acknowledge [Him] and renounce [unbelief] and do good works, [my envoy] shall accept him and help him to [do right], but I have ordered him to fight those who deny [Him] for that reason. So he will not spare any one of them he can gain mastery over, [but may] burn them with fire, slaughter them by any means, and take women and children captive; nor shall he accept from anyone anything except Islam.[176]*

Abu Bakr even set the example when a captive who had fought against the Muslims was brought to him. Abu Bakr

> *ordered a fire to be kindled with much firewood in the prayer yard (musalla) of Medina and threw him, with arms and legs bound, into it.[177]*

The commander of one of the Muslim armies was Khalid bin al-Walid. Here is a command that Abu Bakr gave to Khalid:

> *When you encamp someplace, make the call to prayer and the iqamah. Then, if the people make the call to prayer and the iqamah, leave them alone; but if they do not do so,*

---

[176]   *The History of al-Tabari: The Conquest of Arabia*, p. 57.

[177]   Ibid., p. 80. This incident was also reported in *The Origins of the Islamic State*, p. 149.

there is no [course] but to raid them. [In that case] kill
them by every means, by fire or whatever else.[178]

There was another report about this letter that Abu Bakr sent with Khalid:

I have sent Khalid to you with the Muhajirun and the
Ansar and those who follow them with good conduct. And
I have ordered him not to fight anyone until he has called
him to the worship of Allah; so whoever enters the
religion of Allah and performs righteous deeds, he will
accept that from him, but whoever refuses, he will not
allow him to remain upon that. He will burn them by fire
and take their women and children captive.[179]

And Abu Bakr gave Khalid a specific command when he sent him against the Bani Hanifah in Al-Yamamah:

Then if Allah grants you victory over them, I warn you
against letting them live: Kill their wounded, seek out
those of them who flee, put the captives among them to the
sword and strike terror among them by killing and burn
them by fire. And I warn you against contradicting my
orders. Peace (be upon you).[180]

Khalid took Abu Bakr's words to heart on many occasions during this war. Here is how it was later described:

The outstanding case of apostasy was the secession of the
tribes of Arabia after the death of Muhammad. Abu Bakr,

---

[178]   *The History of al-Tabari: The Conquest of Arabia*, p. 100. The *iqamah* is the second Muslim call to prayer, made just to those gathered inside the mosque immediately before the actual prayer starts.

[179]   *Abridged Biography of Prophet Muhammad*, p. 331.

[180]   Ibid., p. 345.

*the first caliph, warned them first to return to Islam, and
those who did not return were severely fought, especially
by Khalid ibn al-Walid, who burned a great number of
them in spite of objections raised regarding the penalty of
burning. The leaders of the apostate tribes were severely
punished and most of them were slain. An eminent
chronicler, al-Baladhuri, reports that nobody escaped
death save those who returned to Islam.*[181]

Al-Baladuri wrote about one of the battles:

*They fought against Khalid, and one of the Moslems fell a
martyr. By Allah's help at last, the "polytheist" troops
were dispersed, and Khalid had on that day the apostates
burned. When abu-Bakr was told about it, he said, "I
shall not sheathe a sword that Allah had unsheathed
against the 'unbelievers.' "*[182]

And even Ali, the fourth "Rightly Guided" Caliph (656-661), had ordered
people to be burned alive:

*Narrated 'Ikrima: 'Ali burnt some people and this news
reached Ibn 'Abbas, who said, "Had I been in his place I
would not have burnt them, as the Prophet said, 'Don't
punish (anybody) with Allah's punishment.' No doubt, I*

---

[181]   Majid Khadduri, *War and Peace in the Law of Islam* (Clark, NJ: The
Lawbook Exchange Ltd., 2006), p. 77. Khalid ibn al-Walid was known as *The
Sword of Allah.* For other incidents of Khalid capturing apostates and then
burning them alive, see *Abridged Biography of Prophet Muhammad*, pp. 336, and
359-360.

[182]   *The Origins of the Islamic State*, p. 148.

would have killed them, for the Prophet said, 'If somebody (a Muslim) discards his religion, kill him.'"[183]

So we can see that under Islam, there is no general prohibition against burning people alive, even if they are captives.

---

[183]   *Sahih Al-Bukhari*, Vol. 4, Book 56, No. 3017, p. 159; for a similar version see *Sahih Al-Bukhari*, Vol. 9, Book 88, No. 6922, p. 46. This *hadith* was also reported in *Jami' At-Tirmidhi*, with the following modern commentary:

> *The people, who were burnt alive, were the followers of a Jew named 'Abdullah bin Sabah. They were hypocrites and they were involved in a heinous crime of preaching 'Ali's divinity, so 'Ali giving a lesson for others, gave them such a severe punishment.*

Jami' At-Tirmidhi, Vol. 3, Comment to *Hadith* No. 1458, p. 244.

11

The Law of Equality (Qisas)

But even if there were doctrinal prohibitions against the killing of women and children, mutilation of the living, raping of female captives, and the other actions discussed in the previous chapters, under the *Law of Equality (Qisas)* it could be permissible for a Muslim to do any of these things.

Qisas allows for "parity in retaliation," and the basis for it is found in the following verse of the Koran:[184]

Chapter 2, Verse 194

> *The sacred month is for the sacred month, and for the*
> *prohibited things, there is the Law of Equality (Qisas).*
> *Then whoever transgresses the prohibition against you,*
> *you transgress likewise against him. And fear Allah, and*
> *know that Allah is with Al-Muttaqun (the pious).*

So in general, whatever a non-Muslim does against a Muslim becomes permissible for the Muslim to do in retaliation, even if it is technically prohibited under Islam.

---

[184] Abu 'Abdullah Muhammad ibn Ahmad al-Ansari al-Qurtubi, *Tafsir Al-Qurtubi: Classical Commentary of the Holy Qur'an*, Vol. 1, trans. Aisha Bewley (London: Dar Al Taqwa Ltd., 2003), p. 498; and *Tafsir Al-Jalalayn*, p. 70. For other verses in the Koran pertaining to the idea of *Qisas*, see, e.g., 2:178-179, 2:191, 5:45, 16:126, 22:60, and 42:39-41.

This was expounded upon in an essay titled *The Clarification Regarding Intentionally Targetting Women and Children*.[185] This essay addressed some of the topics we have considered in previous chapters:

Mutilation

According to the *Law of Equality*, mutilation can be allowed. The Muslim scholar Ibn Taymiyyah explained,

> *As for mutilation, then it is forbidden, except if it is done for Equal Retaliation. And as 'Imrān ibn Husayn narrated, "The Messenger never gave us a speech, except that he had also ordered us with honesty, and prohibited us from mutilation." And even the kuffār, when we fight against them- we cannot mutilate them, nor cut off their ears, nor disembowel them – unless they do that to us, then we can do to them as they did to us.*[186]

In fact, the following chapter of the Koran was "revealed" with regard to mutilation:[187]

Chapter 16, Verse 126

> *And if you punish (your enemy, O you believers in the Oneness of Allah), then punish them with the like of that*

---

[185]   This essay was mentioned on page 29 of the November 2013 special Westgate Mall edition of *Al-Shabaab's* magazine *Gaidi Mtaani*.

[186]   *The Clarification Regarding Intentionally Targetting Women and Children*, p. 42.

[187]   *Tafsir Al-Jalalayn*, p. 588; *Tafsir Ibn 'Abbas*, p. 346; *Al-Wahidi's Asbab al-Nuzul*, pp. 143-144; and *The Clarification Regarding Intentionally Targetting Women and Children*, pp. 42, and 50-52.

with which you were afflicted. But if you endure patiently,
verily, it is better for As-Sabirun (the patient).

And the Muslim scholar Ibn Al-Qayyim specifically referred to the first part of this verse as justification for mutilation under *The Law of Equality*:

> *Indeed Allāh has permitted the Muslims to mutilate the*
> *kuffār if they mutilate them (i.e. Muslims) - even though*
> *mutilation is forbidden (originally). Allāh (Most High)*
> *says, "And if you punish (your enemy, O you believers in*
> *the Oneness of Allāh), then punish them with the like of*
> *that with which you were afflicted." So this Verse is*
> *evidence that cutting noses and ears, and splitting open*
> *bellies- if done in retaliation- then it is neither a*
> *transgression nor a crime- rather, equal retaliation is*
> *justice.*[188]

The essay quoted additional Muslim scholars who stated that the *Law of Equality* justified the mutilation of non-Muslims.[189]

The idea that mutilation was allowed under the *Law of Equality* was also noted in the modern comments for a *hadith* in which Muhammad was reported as prohibiting mutilation:

> *Mutilating the body of the enemy after death, or mutilating*
> *the face while he lives, are both prohibited in Islam.*
> *Exceptions are in cases of Qisas (legal punishment of*
> *requital).*[190]

---

[188]   *The Clarification Regarding Intentionally Targeting Women and Children*, pp. 53-54.

[189]   Ibid., pp. 52-54.

[190]   *Sunan Abu Dawud*, Vol. 3, Comment to *Hadith* No. 2667, p. 295.

And it is interesting to point out that Muhammad even referred to the *Law of Equality* when talking about specific treatment of a slave:

> *It was narrated from Samurah bin Jundab that the Messenger of Allah said: "Whoever kills his slave, we will kill him, and whoever mutilates (his slave) we will mutilate him."[191]*

Women and Children

The essay repeatedly stated that since the *kuffar* were killing Muslim women and children, how could the *Law of Equality* not be applied to the women and children of the *kuffar*?[192] The essay then referred to numerous Muslim scholars who supported the claim that non-Muslim woman and children could therefore be killed.[193]

This was aptly summed up by Osama Bin Laden in an interview on October 21, 2001:

> *...they say that the Prophet forbade the killing of children and women, and that is true...But this forbidding of killing children and innocents...is not unrestricted [sic] and there are other texts which restrict [sic] it...The scholars and people of knowledge...say that if the disbelievers were to kill our children and women, then we should not feel ashamed to do the same to them, mainly to deter them*

---

[191]   *Sunan Ibn Majah*, Vol. 3, No. 2663, p. 530. For similar versions of this hadith, see: *Jami' At-Tirmidhi*, Vol. 3, No. 1414, p. 198; *Sunan Abu Dawud*, Vol. 5, Nos. 4515-4516, p. 112; and *Sunan An-Nasa'i*, Vol. 5, Nos. 4740-4742, p. 393.

[192]   *The Clarification Regarding Intentionally Targetting Women and Children*, pp. 46-47.

[193]   Ibid., pp. 48-49, 68, 72-73, 83, 89-90, and 94-95.

from trying to kill our children and women again. And that is from a religious standpoint...[194]

The Islamic scholar Ibn Salih Al-'Uthaymin pointed out that killing women and children was allowed even if it meant a loss in *profit* or *benefit* to the Muslims:

> *The apparent [Thahir] is that <u>it is (permissible) for us to kill their women and children</u> [sic] – even if it means that we lose profit/benefit from it [since keeping them alive is a profit/benefit because they become the property of the Muslims]; (and killing them in this situation is permissible) due to it threatening the hearts of the enemies and a humiliation for them.[195]*

At this point you might be asking yourself how the *Law of Equality* could allow the mutilation and/or killing of uninvolved non-combatants?

The answer is to be found in the concept of collective punishment, supported by the following two verses from the Koran:

Chapter 8, Verse 25

> *And fear the Fitnah (affliction and trial) which affects not in particular (only) those of you who do wrong (but it may afflict all the good and the bad people), and know that Allah is Severe in punishment.*

---

194   Ibid., pp. 80-81.

195   Ibid., p. 72.

Chapter 17, Verse 16

> *And when We decide to destroy a town (population), We*
> *(first) send a definite order (to obey Allah and be*
> *righteous) to those among them...Then, they transgress*
> *therein, and thus the word (of torment) is justified against*
> *it (them). Then We destroy it with complete destruction.*

The relevance of these verses was explained by Shaykh Al-Mujahidin
Yusuf Al-'Uyayri, who was killed in 2003 and had been the first leader of
Al-Qaeda on the Arabian Peninsula:

> *...Because these crimes, for which Allah also punishes*
> *those who did not perpetrate them, are transgressions*
> *which implicate the collective group – for indeed the*
> *group was capable, since it was aware that they were*
> *committing crimes, of forcing the perpetrators to refrain*
> *from their crimes. And it is for this reason that the*
> *Shari'ah has brought punishment upon the collective*
> *group on behalf of the individual criminals; so that this*
> *can be an encouragement and motivation for the collective*
> *group to stop the perpetrators before they are all*
> *collectively punished. And Allah knows best.*[196]

And it is not just the Koran that provides support for collective
punishment. The essay points out that numerous Muslim scholars have
mentioned examples of Muhammad engaging in collective punishment:
e.g., killing <u>all</u> of the Jewish males who had reached puberty among the
Bani Qurayzah; the indiscriminate use of a catapult at the siege of al-Ta'if;

---

[196]   Ibid., p. 57. The understanding that these verses referred to collective
punishment of the good people along with the evil is also found in: *Tafsir Ibn
Kathir*, Vol. 4, pp. 288-292; *Tafsir Al-Jalalayn*, pp. 381-382 and 595; *Tafsir
Ahsanul-Bayan*, Vol. 2, p. 283; and Vol. 3, p. 274; and *Tafsir Ibn 'Abbas*, pp. 218-
219 and 350.

and the taking captive of a man whose only crime was that his tribe was allied with a tribe that had captured two Muslims. [197]

It is interesting to note that under certain circumstances, exercising the right of the *Law of Equality* may be declined if, for example, it "would not result in any advance in the *Jihad*" or increase the terror in the enemy; Ibn Taymiyyah explained:

> *Verily, the retaliation in kind is a right for them [Muslims]. So it is permitted for them to perform it in order to restore their morale and to take revenge, yet they may decline it (i.e. this right) when patience is preferable. But this is when the retaliation in kind would not result in any advance in the Jihad and when it would not increase their terror (so as to keep them away) from the likes of that. But if a widespread retaliation in kind would be an invitation for them towards Iman [faith, belief in Islam], or a preventative factor towards their aggression, then in this case, it becomes included in a form of establishing the Hudud (i.e. Islamic legislated punishments) and a (proper) Shari'ah-based Jihad.[198]*

That the Law of Equality was a major rationale for the attack on the Westgate Mall is illustrated by two quotes from the special Westgate Mall edition of *Gaidi Mtaani*:

> *The clock was ticking while the Mujahideen were counting the atrocities committed by the Kenyans and, needless to say, revenge was imperative. Revenge for the massacred men, women and children! Revenge for the raped Muslim women![199]*

---

[197]   *The Clarification Regarding Intentionally Targetting Women and Children*, pp. 55, 70, and 104-105.

[198]   Ibid., p. 53.

[199]   *Gaidi Mtaani*, pp. 14-15.

And

> *It is simple; as you have done unto others, expect them to return the favor in the same measure…As the kuffar intentionally bombed and killed women and children in Mujahideen controlled areas of Somalia, the Mujahideen, justifiably, have the right to kill their women and children, and every action will be met with an appropriate response, even if it comes after a while.*[200]

Conclusion

So this chapter and the preceding seven chapters show us that the attack on the Westgate Mall and the actions of the *Mujahideen* there were not only done in the name of Islam, but supported by Islamic doctrine.

By focusing on the Islam of Muhammad we not only gain a better understanding of the doctrinal bases for particular acts done by *jihadists*, but we can use these eight chapters as models to examine future *jihadist* actions in order to determine their doctrinal basis in Islam.

---

[200]   Ibid., p. 20.

12

Redefining Jihad

There is an effort underway to redefine the meaning of *Jihad* away from the concept of an Islamic holy war against non-Muslims. This effort consists of a two-pronged approach: 1) creating new definitions, and 2) doing away with the old.

Creating New Definitions

The first prong is well demonstrated at a website titled *MyJihad* (http://myjihad.org/), where the stated purpose is,

> *Taking Back Islam from Muslim & anti-Muslim extremists alike.*

As part of this effort, *MyJihad* has been promoting an advertising campaign to place redefining billboards on city buses. Pictures on the website show billboards on buses that redefine *Jihad* in the following ways, with appropriate pictures of individuals to personalize these slogans:

> *My Jihad is to stay fit despite my busy schedule.*

> *My Jihad is to build friendships across the aisle.*[201]

> *My Jihad is to march on despite losing my son.*

---

[201] This is an interesting redefinition when considered with the fact that 5:51 of the Koran specifically prohibits Muslims from being friends with Christians and Jews. And this is just one of many Koranic verses prohibiting Muslims from being friends with non-Muslims.

However, I am more familiar with the following understanding of *Jihad*, found in *The Noble Qur'an*:

> *Al-Jihad (holy fighting) in Allah's Cause (with full force of numbers and weaponry) is given the utmost importance in Islam and is one of its pillars (on which it stands). By Jihad Islam is established, Allah's Word is made superior, (His Word being La ilaha illallah which means none has the right to be worshipped but Allah), and His religion (Islam) is propagated. By abandoning Jihad (may Allah protect us from that) Islam is destroyed and the Muslims fall into an inferior position; their honour is lost, their lands are stolen, their rule and authority vanish. Jihad is an obligatory duty in Islam on every Muslim, and he who tries to escape from this duty, or does not in his innermost heart wish to fulfil [sic] this duty, dies with one of the qualities of a hypocrite.[202]*

I was interested to learn about the doctrinal basis for the new definitions of *Jihad* found at *MyJihad*, so I went to the *Resources* page at that website. After reading through the articles, I found that this attempt to redefine *Jihad* is based largely on three approaches:

1. Using a partially quoted *hadith* taken out of context.

2. Using fabricated or, at best, weak *hadiths*.

3. Using an entire *hadith* taken out of context.

Although we have referred to, and used *hadiths* throughout the preceding chapters, for this chapter we must ensure a basic understanding of the *hadiths*.

---

[202]   *The Noble Qur'an*, n. 1, p. 50. This translation of the Koran was published by Darussalam Publishers in Saudi Arabia. Would this understanding of *Jihad* therefore make the Muslims at Darussalam "extremists" in the eyes of the Muslims at the *MyJihad* website?

So what is a *hadith*? The *hadiths* are reports about the examples, ways, and teachings of Muhammad believed to have come from those who were with him and observed and heard them. They are second only to the Koran in importance to Islam. And the Koran cannot be understood without relying on the *hadiths*.

There are numerous *hadith* collections, with varying degrees of reliability. But there are two collections considered to be the most reliable (*sahih*). The first is *Sahih Al-Bukhari*, collected by Muhammad bin Ismail al-Bukhari (810-870) and considered the most reliable collection of *hadiths*:

> *The authenticity of Al-Bukhari's work is such that the*
> *religious learned scholars of Islam said concerning him:*
> *"The most authentic book after the Book of Allah (i.e. Al-*
> *Qur'an) is Sahih Al-Bukhari."* [203]

The next most reliable *hadith* collection is *Sahih Muslim*, collected by Abu'l Hussain 'Asakir-ud-Din Muslim bin Hajjaj al-Qushayri al-Naisaburi (821-875).

The two *Sahihs* and four other *hadith* collections make up the authoritative "Six Books of *Hadith*," or "The Sound Six." Here are the other four *hadith* collections:

Sunan Ibn Majah - Muhammad bin Yazeed ibn Majah Al-Qazwini (831-895)

Sunan An-Nasa'i - Abu 'Abdur-Rahman Ahmad bin Shu'aib bin 'Ali bin Sinan bin Bahr An-Nasa'i (836-925)

Sunan Abu Dawud - Abu Dawud Sulaiman bin Al-Ash'ath bin Ishaq (824-897)

---

[203]   *Sahih Al-Bukhari*, Vol. 1, p. 18.

Jami' At-Tirmidhi - Abu 'Eisa Mohammad ibn 'Eisa at-Tirmidhi (827-901)

Although designated as the "Six Books," the English translations of these collections total 39 volumes.

It should be noted that Muhammad died in 632, and these *hadith* collections were put together over 200 years later. During the intervening time period, the *hadiths* had been handed down verbally, for the most part, for a number of generations. Nevertheless, these *hadith* collections are among the canonical texts of Islam.

Now let's look at the *hadiths* the *MyJihad* website is relying on to provide new definitions of the meaning of *Jihad*.

1. The Partially Quoted *Hadith* Taken Out of Context

One of the articles on the *Resources* page is titled *The Spiritual Significance of Jihad*. In this article we find the following statement attributed to Muhammad:

> *Nor is the hajj to the centre of the Islamic world in Mecca possible without long preparation, effort, often suffering and endurance of hardship. It requires great effort and exertion so that the Prophet could say, 'The hajj is the most excellent of all jihads".* [sic]

The *Hajj* is the pilgrimage to Mecca that is incumbent on every Muslim to make at least once in their life, if they are able to make it. The *Hajj* can only be taken during a certain time of the year.

However, Muhammad did not say that the *Hajj* was "the most excellent of all jihads." According to our canonical *hadith* collections, Muhammad actually said Hajj was the best *Jihad* <u>for women</u> because there was no fighting involved, e.g.:

1. *Narrated 'Aishah (that she said), "O Allah's Messenger! We consider Jihad as the best deed. Should we not fight in Allah's Cause?" He said, "The best Jihad (for women) is Hajj-Mabrur (i.e., Hajj which is done according to the Prophet's Sunna and is accepted by Allah)."*[204]

2. *It was narrated that 'Aishah said: "I said: 'O Messenger of Allah, is Jihad obligatory for women?' He said: "Yes: Upon them is a Jihad in which there is no fighting: Al-Hajj and Al-'Umrah.*[205]

And Muhammad went even further by saying that *Hajj* and *'Umrah* were also the *Jihad* of the elderly, weak, and young:

> *It was narrated from Abu Hurairah that the Messenger of Allah said: "Jihad of the elderly, the young, the weak, and women, is Hajj and 'Umrah.*[206]

---

[204] *Sahih Al-Bukhari*, Vol. 4, Book 56, No. 2784, p. 45. In another *hadith*, Aisha requested permission from Muhammad "to participate in *Jihad.*" Muhammad told her, "Your *Jihad* is (the performance of) Hajj"; see *Sahih Al-Bukhari*, Vol. 4, Book 56, No. 2875, p. 89. For a *hadith* in which Muhammad told all of his wives that the best *Jihad* for them was to perform the *Hajj*, see *Sahih Al-Bukhari*, Vol. 4, Book 56, No. 2876, pp. 89-90. These last two *hadiths* are in a chapter titled *The Jihad of women.*

[205] *Sunan Ibn Majah*, Vol. 4, No. 2901, p. 126. The modern commentary for this *hadith* stated:

> *Participating in Jihad or fighting is not obligatory on a woman...The importance of Hajj and 'Umrah for women is as the importance of Jihad for men.*

Al-'Umrah is a pilgrimage to Mecca that can be taken anytime of the year.

[206] *Sunan An-Nasa'i*, Vol. 3, No. 2627, p. 420. The modern commentary for this *hadith* explained:

112

One of Muhammad's wives succinctly summed it up:

> It was narrated from Umm Salamah that the Messenger of
> Allah said, "Hajj is the Jihad of every weak person."[207]

These *hadiths* provide the context for the following *hadith*, which would
then pertain only to the elderly, weak, young, and women:

> The Mother of the Believers, 'Aishah, said: "I said: 'O
> Messenger of Allah, shall we not go out and fight in Jihad
> with you, for I do not think there is any deed in the Qur'an
> that is better than Jihad.' He said: 'No, the best and most
> beautiful (type) of Jihad is Hajj to the House; Hajj Al-
> Mabrur.'"[208]

And Al-Bukhari provided a definitive *hadith* showing the relationship of
performing *Jihad* (holy fighting) in Allah's cause to the performance of
Hajj:

> Narrated Abu Hurairah: The Prophet was asked, "Which
> is the best deed?" He said, "To believe in Allah and His

> Obviously, these four kinds of people cannot go to fight in the
> way of Allah. The way to gain the merit of fighting in the way of
> Allah, or Jihad, for them, is that they should perform Hajj and
> 'Umrah. They would gain the reward of Jihad. Each one's
> recompense is proportionate to his capability.

[207] *Sunan Ibn Majah*, Vol. 4, No. 2902, p. 126.

[208] *Sunan An-Nasa'i*, Vol. 3, No. 2629, p. 421. The modern commentary for
this *hadith* explained:

> Primarily, the womenfolk used to accompany the army to
> provide help to the wounded with water, to transport them from
> the battlefield, and give them first aid, and tend to them. But
> when the number of men increased, the common going forth of
> the womenfolk with the army, even for the above-mentioned
> objectives, ceased.

*Messenger (Muhammad)." He was then asked, "Which is
the next (in goodness)?" He said, "To participate in
Jihad in Allah's Cause." He was again asked, "Which is
the next?" He said, "To perform Hajj-Mabrur."*[209]

This was reiterated by the 14th century Islamic scholar ibn Taymiyyah
when he was discussing *Jihad* as meaning to fight in the way of Allah:

*The command to participate in Jihaad and the mention of
its merits occur innumerable times in the Quraan and the
Sunnah. Therefore, it is the best voluntary [religious] act
that man can perform. All scholars agree that it is better
than the hajj (greater pilgrimage) and the 'umrah (lesser
pilgrimage), than voluntary salaah and voluntary fasting,
as the Quraan and the Sunnah indicate.*[210]

What did Muhammad say was the best *Jihad* in general?

*It was narrated that 'Amr bin 'Abasah said: "I came to
the Prophet and said: 'O Messenger of Allah, which Jihad*

---

[209]   *Sahih Al-Bukhari*, Vol. 2, Book 25, No. 1519, p. 345. A similar *hadith*
was reported in *Sunan An-Nasa'i*, Vol. 3, No. 2625, p. 419; and *Sahih Muslim*,
Vol. 1, No. 83, p. 57.

[210]   Shaykh ul-Islaam Taqi ud-Deen Ahmad ibn Taymiyyah, *The Religious
and Moral Doctrine of Jihaad* (Birmingham, England: Maktabah Al Ansaar
Publications, 2001), p. 25. Accessed on April 15, 2014 at

   http://islamfuture.files.wordpress.com/2009/11/the-religious-and-moral-
   doctrine-of-jihaad.pdf.

A version of this statement, with the same understanding about the superiority of
Jihad (fighting in Allah's cause), is found in Sheikh 'Abdullah bin Muhammad
bin Humaid, "The Call to Jihad (Fighting For Allah's Cause) in the Qur'an," *The
Noble Qur'an*, trans. Muhammad Muhsin Khan and Muhammad Taqi-ud-Din Al-
Hilali (Riyadh, Kingdom of Saudi Arabia: Maktaba Dar-us-Salam, 1994), p. 1052.

114

is best'? He said: '(That of a man) whose blood is shed and his horse is wounded.'"[211]

So the best *Jihad* is to fight and shed blood in the cause of Allah.

We can see the claim that Muhammad said that *Hajj* was "the most excellent of all *jihads*" appears to be based, at best, on a partially quoted *hadith* taken out of context.

2. Lesser *Jihad* and Greater *Jihad*

Two articles on the *MyJihad* website rely on purported statements made by Muhammad that distinguished between a *Lesser Jihad* and a *Greater Jihad*.

Here is how it is presented in the first article, *Jihad against the Abuse of Jihad*, by Abukar Arman:

> *Indeed it is this latter aspect, the jihad with oneself as one resists temptations and strives against his/her evil tendencies, which Prophet Muhammad referred to as "the Greater Jihad," because purification of the soul or simply self-purification is an around-the-clock process in which one engages in a steadfast introspection.*

And here is what is said in the second article, *The Spiritual Significance of Jihad*, by Seyyed Hossein Nasr:

> *You have returned from the lesser jihad to the greater jihad. (Hadith)*
>
> *...But it was upon returning from one of these early wars, which was of paramount importance in the survival of the*

---

[211]   *Sunan Ibn Majah*, Vol. 4, No. 2794, p. 65.

newly established religious community and therefore of
cosmic significance, that the Prophet nevertheless said to
his companions that they had returned from the lesser
holy war to the greater holy war, the greater jihad being
the inner battle against all the forces which would prevent
man from living according to the theomorphic norm which
is his primordial and God given nature.

Are there authoritative sources for this purported distinction made by
Muhammad?

One of the places in which this distinction is found is a book titled
*Reliance of the Traveller (Umdat al-Salik), A Classic Manual of Islamic
Sacred Law.* This is an English translation of a 14th century Shafi'i manual
of Sharia Law. Here is the statement found in that book that Muhammad
purportedly made on returning from *Jihad* (battle):

> *We have returned from the lesser jihad to the greater
> jihad.*[212]

But it is essential to note that this statement and the context for it are not in
the actual text of the 14th century Shafi'i manual. Rather, they are part of
the commentary written for *Reliance of the Traveller* by Sheikh 'Umar
Barakat ibn al-Sayyid, a noted Shafi'i scholar who lived in the 19th century;
here is Barakat's commentary:

> *Jihad means to war against non-Muslims, and is
> etymologically derived from the word mujahada,
> signifying warfare to establish the religion. And it is the
> lesser jihad. As for the greater jihad, it is spiritual
> warfare against the lower self (nafs), which is why the
> Prophet (Allah bless him and give him peace) said as he
> was returning from jihad,*

---

[212]   *Reliance of the Traveller*, o9.0.

"We have returned from the lesser jihad to the greater jihad."[213]

This distinction between a lesser and a greater *Jihad* was also reported in a second *hadith*; the version below is from a book titled *Minhaj Al-Muslim* (The Way of a Muslim), originally published in 1964:

> *The Prophet came back from a war expedition and said: You all have come with the best arrival, and you have come from the minor Jihad to the major Jihad. He then said: It is the striving of the servant against his desires.[214]*

However, over the centuries Muslim scholars have argued against the validity of these *hadiths* and others in which Muhammad supposedly distinguished between a lesser and a greater *Jihad*. For example, the Islamic scholar Ibn Taymiyah (1263–1328 AD) stated,

> *The hadith of "We returned from the minor Jihad to the major Jihad" is fabricated and is not narrated by any of the scholars who have knowledge of the words of Rasulullah* [Muhammad], *his actions and his Jihad against the nonbelievers. In fact Jihad against Kufar*

---

[213]   Ibid. What appears to be overlooked by many is that the commentary preceding the *lesser jihad/greater jihad* statement supposedly made by Muhammad begins with: *(O: Jihad means to war against non-Muslims...* The commentary continues onto the next page and ends with: *...and these were forty-seven in number.).* The introduction to *Reliance of the Traveller* points out that commentary by Barakat is indicated "by parentheses and the capital letter *O.*" See p. ix. So what many people quote as coming from the book *Reliance of the Traveller* is actually commentary inserted hundreds of years later by Barakat.

[214]   Abu Bakr Jabir Al-Jaza'iry, *Minhaj Al-Muslim*, Vol. 2, (Riyadh, Kingdom of Saudi Arabia: Darussalam, 2001), n. 1, p. 167.

[unbelief] *is among the greatest of deeds. Indeed it is the greatest voluntary deed a human could do.*[215]

In 1964, the author of *Minhaj Al-Muslim* pointed out that the second *hadith* mentioned above, and included in his book, was a "weak" *hadith.*[216]

In 1999, Abu Fadl wrote an article titled *Greater and Lesser Jihad.* In this article he pointed out that the *hadiths* distinguishing between a lesser and a greater *Jihad* "are weak if not false *Hadith.*"[217]

A 2002 book on Islamic sacred law came down on the side of those who said these *Lesser and Greater Jihad hadiths* were fabricated:

> *This phrase has become widespread, mentioned both in gatherings and in print, yet despite its popularity in terms of how often it is quoted, it cannot correctly be attributed to the Prophet.*[218]

---

[215]   Abi Zakaryya al-Dimashqi al-Dumyati "ibn-Nuhaas," *The Book of Jihad (Abridged)*, trans. Noor Yamani, revised by Abu Rauda, (no publisher information, 2005), p. 10. This book was written circa 1409 AD and is available online at numerous websites. The book used here was downloaded on April 19, 2013 from *Islamic e Books* at http://islamic-e-books.com/Book_of_Jihad.

[216]   *Minhaj Al-Muslim*, Vol. 2, n. 1, p. 167.

[217]   *The Book of Jihad (Abridged)*, p. 175. This article can also be found at a number of Muslim websites, e.g.,

1.   http://muslimvillage.com/forums/topic/966-the-greater-lesser-jihad/
2.   http://easydeen.wordpress.com/2012/04/23/greater-lesser-jihad/
3.   http://www.geocities.ws/korn14w4n/artikel_2/159.htm

[218]   *Fatawa Islamiyah, Islamic Verdicts*, Vol. 7, collected by Muhammad bin 'Abdul-'Aziz al-Musnad, (Riyadh, Kingdom of Saudi Arabia: Darussalam, 2002), pp. 202-203.

And there are numerous Muslim websites that state these particular *hadiths* are weak or fabricated.[219]

This issue was addressed in more general terms in a 2003 article titled *39 Ways to Serve and Participate in Jihad*:

> *And when the word 'Jihad' is mentioned, it refers to qital* [fighting], *as Ibn Rushd said: "...and when the word 'Jihad" is mentioned, it means physically fighting the disbelievers with the sword until they submit or give the Jizyah by their hands while they are in a state of humiliation..."*
>
> *So, it is not for anyone to generalize this word to include striving against the soul (Jihad an-Nafs) or by the tongue or pen, or calling to Allah (Da'wah). It is true that these actions are actions of piety and obedience to Allah, but they are not intended by the word Jihad in the texts of Islamic law except when it is specified to mean these things.*[220]

---

[219]   For example:

1.   http://www.islamicboard.com/miscellaneous/134296653-one-really-famous-hadith-actually-fake-lesser-vs-greater-jihaad.html
2.   http://muslimvillage.com/forums/topic/966-the-greater-lesser-jihad/
3.   http://www.sunniforum.com/forum/showthread.php?32247-Jihad-against-the-Desires/page3
4.   http://al-qimmah.net/showthread.php?p=12972&langid=2
5.   http://easydeen.wordpress.com/2012/04/23/greater-lesser-jihad/

[220]   Muhammad bin Ahmad as-Salim ('Isa al-'Awshin), *39 Ways to Serve and Participate in Jihad*, At-Tibyan Publications, July 19, 2003, p. 11. Accessed on December 17, 2013 at:

https://ia600408.us.archive.org/7/items/39WaysToServeAndParticipate/39 WaysToServeAndParticipateInJihad.pdf.

119

If Muhammad had actually referred to the personal struggle to better oneself as the *Greater Jihad*, we should certainly find such a *hadith* in the canonical *hadith* collections mentioned earlier. Each of these six collections has a chapter or chapters focusing on *Jihad*. I went through each of those chapters and categorized the *hadiths* under three headings:

1. Fighting in the Cause of Allah/Battle Related – these *hadiths* specifically referred to fighting against non-Muslims or other battle-related activities.

2. Miscellaneous – these *hadiths* made no reference to *Jihad* or battle. The topics covered by these *hadiths* included such things as horse racing, the color of horses, wills and inheritance, hunting, travelling alone, and seasickness.

3. Personal Struggle – any *hadith* equating *Jihad* with the personal struggle to better oneself.

The chart on the next page shows the results of this inquiry. Of the 1,148 *hadiths* I reviewed, 847 pertained to fighting in the cause of Allah (*Jihad*), 301 dealt with miscellaneous topics, and none pertained to a personal struggle to better oneself.

Six Books of Hadith

	Fighting in the Cause of Allah/Battle Related	Miscellaneous No Jihad/Battle	Personal Struggle
Sahih Al-Bukhari The Book of *Jihad*	205	106	0
Sahih Muslim Book of the Holy Struggle (The Book of *Jihad* and Expedition)**	148	36	0
Sunan Abu Dawud The Book of *Jihad*	219	92	0
Jami' At-Tirmidhi Chapters on the Virtue of *Jihad* Chapters on *Jihad*	72	29	0
Sunan An-Nasa'i The Book of *Jihad*	104	7	0
Sunan Ibn Majah Chapters on Jihad	99	31	0
Total Number of *Hadiths* :	**847**	**301**	**0**

**So titled at the website for the Center for Muslim-Jewish Engagement, University of Southern California - http://www.usc.edu/org/cmje/religious-texts/hadith/muslim/019-smt.php

I then decided to take the same approach and review books from the four major Sunni schools of Sharia Law (Islamic Sacred Law). Each of the four books[221] has a chapter focusing on *Jihad*. Because not all of these four books relied exclusively on *hadiths*, I counted the number of pages devoted to each of the three headings. The chart below shows the results. As with the canonical *hadith* collections, the majority of pages were

---

[221]   1) *The Kitab al-Athar of Imam Abu Hanifah*; 2) *Reliance of the Traveller*; 3) *Al-Muwatta of Imam Malik ibn Anas*; 4) and Imam Muwaffaq ad-Din Abdu'llah ibn Ahmad ibn Qudama al-Maqdisi, *The Mainstay Concerning Jurisprudence (Al-Umda fi 'l-Fiqh)*, trans. Muhtar Holland (Ft. Lauderdale, FL: Al-Baz Publishing, Inc., 2009).

devoted to *Jihad* as meaning to fight in the cause of Allah, while none pertained to a personal struggle to better oneself.

Four Major Sunni Schools
of Sharia Law

	Fighting in the Cause of Allah/Battle Related	Miscellaneous No Jihad/Battle	Personal Struggle
Hanafi *The Kitab al-Athar of Imam Abu Hanifah* Chapter 281: *Jihad*	7	0	0
Shafi'i *Reliance of the Traveller (Umdat al-Salik)* Chapter o9.0: *Jihad*	6	0	0
Maliki *Al-Muwatta of Imam Malik ibn Anas* Chapter 21: *Jihad*	43	9	0
Hanbali *The Mainstay Concerning Jurisprudence* Chapter: *The Book of the Holy War* *(Kitab al-Jihad)*	10	0	0
Total Number of Pages:	66	9	0

It appears that among these canonical books and writings of Muslim scholars there is no support for the idea that Muhammad differentiated between a *Lesser Jihad* and a *Greater Jihad*, with the latter being a form of personal struggle. The focus of these works is on the idea that *Jihad* means to fight in the cause of Allah against non-Muslims. And any purported distinction made by Muhammad between a lesser and a greater *Jihad* is based at best on weak evidence, but is most likely fabricated.

But what would Muhammad say on returning from a battle? *Sahih Al-Bukhari* provides us the following *hadith* in a chapter titled, "What to say on returning from *Jihad*":

> *Narrated 'Abdullah: When the Prophet returned (from Jihad), he would say Takbir [Allahu Akbar] thrice and add, "We are returning, if Allah wills, with repentance and worshipping and praising (our Lord) and prostrating ourselves before our Lord. Allah fulfilled His Promise, granted victory to His slave, and He Alone defeated the Ahzab (Confederates)."*[222]

Ibn Kathir reported a variation of this *hadith*:

> *Abdullah Ibn 'Umar also narrated that whenever the Messenger of Allah would return from a battle or Hajj or 'Umrah, he would say Allahu Akbar thrice, then he would say: "There is no diety [sic] worthy of worship except Allah alone without a partner, for Him is the kingdom, for Him is All Praise, and He is able to do all things, returning repenters, worshippers, those who prostrate to our Lord praising, Allah affirmed his promise, and He helped his slave and He defeated the armies Himself."*[223]

Nothing about a lesser or a greater *Jihad* here.

---

[222]   *Sahih Al-Bukhari*, Vol. 4, Book 56, No. 3084, p. 196. A similar *hadith* was reported in *Sunan Abu Dawud*, Vol. 3, No. 2770, pp. 362-363. *Allahu Akbar* means *Allah is greatest*.

[223]   *Winning the Hearts and Souls*, p. 357. A similar version of this *hadith* was reported in *Jami At-Tirmidhi*, Vol. 2, No. 950, pp. 349-350; and *Al-Muwatta of Imam Malik ibn Anas*, 20.81.252.

3. An Additional *Hadith* Taken Out of Context

Prominent on the website pages of *MyJihad* is the following quote attributed to Muhammad:

> *The Best Jihad is a Word of Justice to an Unjust Ruler.*

Here is the *hadith* in which it is found:

> *It was narrated from Abu Sa'eed Al-Khudri that the Messenger of Allah said: "The best of Jihad is a just word spoken to an unjust ruler.*[224]

And here is the modern commentary about this *hadith* to provide its context:

> *An unfair Muslim king is not fought as non-Muslims are fought. So, preaching the truth to him without raising arms against him is a more daring act since such a king either kills him or punishes him severely after imprisoning him.*[225]

So according to this commentary, the use of the phrase *unjust ruler* is actually referring to an *unfair Muslim king.*

This *hadith* was also reported with this wording:

> *It was narrated that Abu Sa'eed Al-Khurdi* [sic] *said: "The Messenger of Allah said: 'The best of Jihad is a just word spoken to an oppressive Sultan" or "an oppressive Amir."*[226]

---

[224]   *Sunan Ibn Majah*, Vol. 5, No. 4011, p. 217.

[225]   Ibid., Comment to *Hadith* No. 4011, p. 217.

[226]   *Sunan Abu Dawud*, Vol. 4, No. 4344, p. 542.

The words *Sultan* and *Amir* refer to Muslim leaders. So with these two *hadiths* we can see that the context of Muhammad's statement referred to confronting an unjust, and/or oppressive Muslim ruler.

This *hadith* is also found in *Jami' At-Tirmidhi*:

> *Abu Sa'eed Al-Khudri narrated that the Prophet said: "Indeed, among the greatest types of Jihad is a just statement before a tyrannical ruler."*[227]

The modern commentary for this *hadith* provides the following explanation:

> *The expression 'Kalimat Al-'Adl' (just statement) as used here, means commanding what is good and prohibiting what is evil. To enjoin good to a tyrannical ruler or prohibit him from doing wrong is inviting disaster for oneself, nay perhaps signing one's own death warrant, while going out to face an enemy is not necessarily to court injury or death. That is why admonishing a tyrannical ruler has been described in the Hadith as the highest form of Jihad.*[228]

The use of the word *Kalimat* is instructive. *Kalimat* means "words" in the sense of "what Allah has willed," or "Allah's Law."[229] So this *hadith* is talking about reminding a tyrannical Muslim ruler about Allah's Law. The message of this *hadith* comes in the context of confronting not just any ruler, but rather a Muslim ruler.

But the *MyJihad* website refers to a generic, non-denominational, "unjust" ruler, which, without understanding the context of the statement, makes it

---

[227]   *Jami' At-Tirmidhi*, Vol. 4, No. 2174, p. 233.

[228]   Ibid., Comment to *Hadith* No. 2174, p. 233.

[229]   *Tafsir Ibn Kathir*, Vol. 1, p. 368.

sound like it could be any ruler who, for example, is simply playing favorites among the people. But Muhammad spoke about this in terms of a tyrannical, oppressive, unjust <u>Muslim</u> ruler. And it was by confronting such a Muslim ruler that one was inviting death, imprisonment with severe punishment, and/or "disaster for oneself."

In contrast, the wording of this *hadith* on the *MyJihad* website makes one think about the relationship that appeared to exist between Mahatma Gandhi and the British rulers of India in the early 20th century. This relationship allowed Gandhi to engage in passive resistance against the perceived injustices of British rule, while knowing that he was probably not signing his "death warrant" by doing so. Zareer Masani aptly noted that this passive resistance by Gandhi

> *could only succeed against a regime which, however*
> *unjust, had a moral conscience and some respect for*
> *individual freedom and the rule of law. It would have*
> *been as useless in Hitler's Germany or Stalin's Russia as*
> *it was in Tiananmen Square.*[230]

It would also have been useless against the kind of unjust Muslim ruler to whom Muhammad was actually referring.

So in the effort to redefine *Jihad*, the *MyJihad* website has taken this *hadith* out of context and used it in a way that implies that the *Best Jihad* could include speaking up to rulers who have a moral conscience and some respect for individual freedom and the rule of law. In contrast, what Muhammad meant was that the *Best of Jihad* consisted of speaking up against unjust <u>Muslim</u> rulers who have no such qualities, and therefore inviting self-destruction in doing so. This shows a stark difference between the *MyJihad* supporters and the Messenger of Allah in understanding the nature of the *Best Jihad*.

---

[230]   Zareer Masani, "The Making of the Mahatma," *Standpoint*, October 2013, p. 57.

Unfortunately, the difference between how this *hadith* is presented on the *MyJihad* website and what Muhammad really meant by it is just a continuation of the current effort to try to redefine the meaning of *Jihad* away from any form of physical violence related to Islam.

Doing Away With The Old

This second prong is best exemplified by what I call the "disappearing Appendix." In the 1994 edition of *The Noble Qur'an* there is a 22-page essay titled "The Call to Jihad (Fighting For Allah's Cause) in the Qur'an."[231] The essay was written by Sheikh 'Abdullah bin Muhammad bin Humaid, of *Al-Masjid-al-Haram* (the Grand Mosque) in Mecca.

Sheikh 'Abdullah was no ordinary sheikh. He was born in 1908 in Riyadh. He memorized the Koran as a youth and studied under renowned sheikhs of Islam. In his adult years he was chosen to head the supervision of religious affairs at the Grand Mosque in Mecca; he also taught there and issued *fatwas* (Islamic legal judgments, issued by an expert in Islamic religious law). In 1974, the king of Saudi Arabia appointed him as head of the Senior Judiciary Committee, a member of the Council of Senior Scholars, the head of the Jurisprudence Committee, and a member of the Foundation Committee for the Muslim World League. The Sheikh died in 1981.[232]

Considering his knowledge and background, it is interesting to note that the Sheikh's essay was not included in the 2003 edition of *The Noble Qur'an*, even though it was listed in the Table of Contents as *Appendix III*

---

[231]   "The Call to Jihad (Fighting For Allah's Cause) in the Qur'an," p. 1043. In the Table of Contents of this edition of *The Noble Qur'an* (p. *v*) this essay was listed as "16. *Jihad.*"

[232]   *Fatwa-Online.com* website accessed on April 18, 2014: http://www.fatwa-online.com/scholarsbiographies/15thcentury/ibnhumayd.htm.

– The Call to Jihad in the Qur'an.[233] And in the 2007 edition of *The Noble Qur'an*, not only was the sheikh's essay not included, it was no longer even mentioned in the Table of Contents![234]

So what did this now-excluded essay say? The Sheikh started out by proclaiming that Allah "has ordained 'Al-Jihad' (Fighting for Allah's Cause)" with the heart (intentions or feelings), the hand (weapons, etc.) and the tongue (speeches, etc., in the cause of Allah). He said that at first "the fighting" had been forbidden by Allah. Then Allah permitted it and later made it obligatory. After "the fighting" had been made obligatory,

> *Then Allah revealed in Sura Tauba...* [Chapter Nine of the Koran] *the order to discard (all) the obligations (covenants, etc.) and commanded the Muslims to fight against all the Mushrikun as well as against the people of the Scriptures (Jews and Christians) if they do not embrace Islam, till they pay the Jizya (a tax levied on the Jews and Christians who do not embrace Islam and are under the protection of an Islamic government) with willing submission and feel themselves subdued (as it is revealed in the Verse 9:29). So they (Muslims) were not permitted to abandon "the fighting" against them (Pagans, Jews and Christians) and to reconcile with them and to suspend hostilities against them for an unlimited period while they (Muslims) are able to fight against them (non Muslims)* [sic].[235]

---

[233]   *The Noble Qur'an*, trans. Muhammad Muhsin Khan and Muhammad Taqi-ud-Din Al-Hilali (Riyadh, Kingdom of Saudi Arabia: Darussalam, 2003); see p. 12 for the Table of Contents.

[234]   *The Noble Qur'an* (2007); see p. 10 for the Table of Contents.

[235]   "The Call to Jihad (Fighting For Allah's Cause) in the Qur'an," pp. 1045-1046. Here is Verse 9:29:

> *Fight against those who believe not in Allah, nor in the Last Day, nor forbid that which has been forbidden by Allah and His*

The Sheikh then made an important point:

> *Allah made "the fighting" (Jihad) obligatory for the Muslims and gave importance to the subject-matter of Jihad in all the Surahs (Chapters of the Qur'an) which were revealed (at Al-Madina)...[236]*

So the importance of *Jihad* (fighting non-Muslims) is found in the chapters of the Koran that were revealed in Medina; these chapters include the generally unabrogated, last verses to be revealed, and the Sheikh quoted liberally from those verses.

The Sheikh referred to *Jihad* as both "Islamic holy war" and "the holy Muslim warfare;" he said that, "Allah will establish His Religion (Islam), with them (*Mujahidin*)."[237]

And the Sheikh explained how Allah felt about the *Mujahidin* in comparison to those Muslims who did not fight:

> *So He (the All-Mighty) denied the equality between the believers who sit (at home) and join not in Jihad – and the Mujahidin (those who fight in Allah's cause), - Then He mentioned the superiority of the Mujahidin over those (believers) who sit (at home) by a grade and then later on mentioned their (Mujahidin's) superiority over them (believers who sit at home) by degrees of grades.[238]*

Messenger (Muhammad), and those who acknowledge not the religion of truth (i.e. Islam) among the people of the Scripture (Jews and Christians), until they pay the Jizyah with willing submission, and feel themselves subdued.

[236] "The Call to Jihad (Fighting For Allah's Cause) in the Qur'an," p. 1046.

[237] Ibid. *Mujahidin* are Muslim warriors engaged in *Jihad*.

[238] Ibid., p. 1049.

He said that Allah disapproved of giving up *Jihad*:

> *Similarly, Allah disapproved of those who abandoned*
> *Jihad (i.e. they did not go for Jihad) and attributed to*
> *them hypocrisy and disease in their hearts, and threatened*
> *(all) those who remain behind from Jihad and sit (at*
> *home) with horrible punishement* [sic]. *He (Allah)*
> *accused them with the most ugly descriptions, rebuked*
> *them for their cowardice and spoke against them (about*
> *their weakness and their remaining behind)...*[239]

Sheikh 'Abdullah added that there were many verses in the Koran that threatened the Muslim nation if they gave up *Jihad*. And he said there was no other organization that compared to Islam in terms of ordering the mobilization of a whole nation to engage in *Jihad* to make the Word of Allah superior:

> *And you will not find any organization past or present,*
> *religious or non-religious as regards (Jihad and military)*
> *(ordering) the whole nation to march forth and mobilize*
> *all of them into active military service as a single row for*
> *Jihad in Allah's Cause so as to make superior the Word of*
> *Allah (i.e. none has the right to be worshipped but Allah),*
> *as you will find in the Islamic Religion and its*
> *teachings.*[240]

The Sheikh also pointed out the Muhammad "has put *Jihad* at the top in Islam."[241]

With a doctrinally sound understanding of *Jihad* like this, it would come as no surprise if those wishing to create new definitions of *Jihad* might be

---

[239]   Ibid., p. 1054.

[240]   Ibid.

[241]   Ibid., p. 1053.

quite happy to do away with essays such as this one by Sheikh 'Abdullah bin Muhammad.

Conclusion

We can see that the *hadiths* mentioned above from the *MyJihad* website tend more to misdirect than to help us in understanding what Muhammad fundamentally meant when he used the term *Jihad*. Allah's and Muhammad's understandings of what *Jihad* means were much better presented in the essay by Sheikh 'Abdullah bin Muhammad, but this essay was omitted from newer versions of *The Noble Qur'an*.

So to establish what Muhammad meant by *Jihad*, let's look at a few *sahih hadiths*:

> *Narrated Abu Hurairah: The Prophet said, "Allah assigns for a person who participates in (holy battles) in Allah's Cause and nothing causes him to do so except belief in Allah and in His Messengers, that he will be recompensed by Allah either with a reward, or booty (if he survives) or will be admitted to Paradise (if he is killed in the battle as a martyr)." The Prophet added: "Had I not found it difficult for my followers, then I would not remain behind any Sariya (an army-unit) going for Jihad and I would have loved to be martyred in Allah's Cause and then made alive, and then martyred and then made alive, and then again martyred in His Cause.*[242]

This *hadith* from *Sahih Al-Bukhari* is found in a chapter titled "*Al-Jihad* (holy fighting in Allah's Cause) is a part of faith." The footnote for this chapter title provides virtually the same understanding of *Al-Jihad* as *The*

---

[242]   *Sahih Al-Bukhari*, Vol. 1, Book 2, No. 36, pp. 72-73.

Noble Qur'an's understanding of *Al-Jihad* that I noted at the beginning of this current chapter.[243]

And in the next *hadith*, Muhammad said that the only deed equal to the Muslim warrior fighting in *Jihad* would be if one could unceasingly perform prayer and fasting as long as the warrior was away – an impossible task:

> *Narrated Abu Hurairah: A man came to Allah's Messenger and said, "Guide me to such a deed as equals Jihad (in reward)." He replied, "I do not find such a deed." Then he added, "Can you, while the Muslim fighter has gone for Jihad enter your mosque to perform Salat (prayer) without cease and observe Saum (fast) and never break your Saum?" The man said, "But who can do that?" Abu Hurairah added, "The Mujahid (i.e., Muslim fighter) is rewarded even for the footsteps of his horse while it wanders about (for grazing) tied in a long rope."[244]*

And here is another *hadith* from *Sahih Al-Bukhari*, found in a chapter titled, "Paradise is under the blades of swords (*Jihad* in Allah's Cause)":

> *Narrated 'Abdullah bin Abi Aufa: Allah's Messenger said, "Know that Paradise is under the shades of swords (Jihad in Allah's Cause)."[245]*

And here is a *hadith* from *Sahih Muslim*:

> *It has been narrated on the authority of Abu Huraira that the Messenger of Allah (may peace be upon him) said:*

---

[243] Ibid., n. 1, p. 72.

[244] Ibid., Vol. 4, Book 56, No. 2785, pp. 45-46.

[245] Ibid., No. 2818, p. 63.

132

*One who died but did not fight in the way of Allah nor did
he express any desire (or determination) for Jihad died
the death of a hypocrite.*[246]

So Muhammad said that one who did not fight in the way of Allah nor
express any desire for such fighting died the death of a hypocrite. And
hypocrisy on the part of a Muslim means acting in contradiction to the
doctrines of Islam.

In these *hadiths* Muhammad is telling us that *Jihad* is an integral part of
Islam, and *Jihad* means engaging in battle against the non-Muslims and
fighting in the way of Allah; it is not a personal struggle to better oneself,
despite the personal perspectives on display at the *MyJihad* website.

We will close this chapter with an apt quote from a modern, award
winning biography of Muhammad:

> *A "war" in Islam is a Jihad. That is to say it is a noble
> sacred fight in the way of Allah for the verification of a
> Muslim society that seeks to free man from cruelty,
> oppression and aggression.*[247]

---

[246]   *Sahih Muslim*, Vol. 6, No. 1910, p. 289. In *Sunan An-Nasa'i* there is
another version of this *hadith* reported under the heading *Stern Warning Against
Forsaking Jihad*:

> *It was narrated from Abu Hurairah that the Prophet said:
> "Whoever dies without having fought or having thought of
> fighting, he dies on one of the branches of hypocrisy.*

Sunan An-Nasa'i, Vol. 4, No. 3099, p. 22.

[247]   *The Sealed Nectar*, p. 514.

13

Islam Teaches Personal Deception

There are two specific verses in the Koran that allow individual Muslims to deceive non-Muslims if the circumstances demand it. The first verse, 3:28, allows Muslims to pretend to be friends with non-Muslims, even though there are many verses in the Koran prohibiting such friendship. The second verse, 16:106, allows Muslims to publically renounce Islam, even though Muhammad said that anyone leaving Islam should be killed. Let's look at the first of these two verses.

Numerous verses in the Koran prohibit Muslims from being friends with non-Muslims. One of the clearest examples of these verses is:

Chapter 5, Verse 51

> *O you who believe! Take not the Jews and the Christians*
> *as Auliya' (friends, protectors, helpers), they are but*
> *Auliya' of each other. And if any amongst you takes them*
> *as Auliya', then surely, he is one of them. Verily, Allah*
> *guides not those people who are the Zalimun (polytheists*
> *and wrongdoers and unjust).*

In a section titled *The Prohibition of Taking the Jews, Christians and Enemies of Islam as Friends*, Ibn Kathir explained this verse by pointing out that

> *Allah forbids His believing servants from having Jews and*
> *Christians as friends, because they are the enemies of*
> *Islam and its people, may Allah curse them. Allah then*
> *states that they are friends of each other and He gives a*

warning threat to those who do this, And if any among you befriends them, then surely he is one of them.[248]

The *Tafsir Al-Jalalayn* explained that this verse meant Muslims were not to join Jews and Christians "in mutual friendship and love," or "in their unbelief."[249]

The *Tafsir Ibn 'Abbas* stated that Muslims who take Jews and Christians as friends are "not included in Allah's protection and safety."[250]

The modern *Tafsir Ahsanul-Bayan* agreed with these interpretations:

> *The verse forbids Muslims to keep intimate relations with them and take them as protectors and helpers, because they are the enemies of Allah, the Muslims, and Islam. It should be noted that those who take them as protectors and helpers will be considered among them.*[251]

Allah's command could not be more unambiguous. So how can one explain an apparently devout Muslim being friends with non-Muslims?

---

[248]   *Tafsir Ibn Kathir*, Vol. 3, p. 204. For examples of other verses in the Koran which prohibit Muslims from taking non-Muslims in general as friends, and/or show a hostile attitude toward non-Muslims, see 2:105, 2:193, 2:221, 3:118, 4:89, 4:101 (*the disbelievers are ever to you open enemies*), 4:139-140, 4:144, 5:55, 5:57, 8:12-13, 8:22, 8:39, 8:59-60, 8:73, 9:5, 9:23, 9:28, 9:29, 9:30, 9:73, 9:123, 13:18, 13:41, 21:44, 47:4, 47:35, 58:22, 60:1, 60:10, 60:13, 66:9, and 68:35. And 48:29 is quite clear:

> *Muhammad is the Messenger of Allah. And those who are with him are severe against disbelievers, and merciful among themselves.*

[249]   *Tafsir Al-Jalalayn*, p. 256.

[250]   *Tafsir Ibn 'Abbas*, p. 143.

[251]   *Tafsir Ahsanul-Bayan*, Vol. 1, p. 616.

The answer can be found in the following verse:

Chapter 3, Verse 28

> *Let not the believers take the disbelievers as Auliya*
> *(supporters, helpers) instead of the believers, and whoever*
> *does that, will never be helped by Allah in any way, except*
> *if you indeed fear a danger from them. And Allah warns*
> *you against Himself (His punishment), and to Allah is the*
> *final return.*

Ibn Kathir explained this verse and the exception it mentioned:

> *Allah prohibited His believing servants from becoming*
> *supporters of the disbelievers, or to take them as*
> *comrades with whom they develop friendships, rather than*
> *the believers...except those believers who in some areas or*
> *times fear for their safety from the disbelievers. In this*
> *case, such believers are allowed to show friendship to the*
> *disbelievers outwardly, but never inwardly. For instance,*
> *Al-Bukhari recorded that Abu Ad-Darda' said, "We smile*
> *in the face of some people although our hearts curse*
> *them." Al-Bukhari said that Al-Hasan said, "The Tuqyah*
> *is allowed until the Day of Resurrection."*[252]

---

[252] *Tafsir Ibn Kathir*, Vol. 2, pp. 141-142; n. 2 on p. 142 defines *Tuqyah*
(*Taqiyya*) as "To shield what is in one's heart." It is also defined as "Concealing
identity"; see Mahmoud Ismail Saleh, *Dictionary of Islamic Words &*
Expressions, 3rd ed. (Riyadh, Kingdom of Saudi Arabia: Darussalam, 2011), p.
237.

For an informative article discussing the significance of *Taqiyya* to Islam, see
Raymond Ibrahim, "How Taqiyya Alters Islam's Rules of War, Defeating Jihadist
Terrorism," *The Middle East Quarterly*, Volume 17, No. 1 (Winter 2010). This
article is accessible at http://www.meforum.org/2538/taqiyya-islam-rules-of-war.

The *Tafsir Al-Jalalayn* explained the exception allowed in this verse:

> ...*unless it is dissimulation out of fear of them so that the befriending takes place with the tongue alone and not the heart. This was before Islam became mighty, when Islam had no power in the land.*[253]

The *Tafsir Ibn 'Abbas* presented a similar explanation:

> ...*saving yourselves from them by speaking in a friendly way towards them with* [sic], *while your hearts dislikes* [sic] *this.*[254]

The modern *Tafsir Ahsanul-Bayan* explained:

> *In this verse, Allah has strictly forbidden the believers to make friends with disbelievers, because the latter are the enemies of Allah as well as enemies of the believers. Hence, there is no reason to make friends with them. There are many verses in the Qur'an warning believers against making friends with disbelievers, except for reasons of expediency or need or trade. Treaties and pacts of mutual benefit may also be concluded with them...because all these are quite different things and have nothing to do with friendship.*[255]

Our modern *tafsir* then explained the exception:

---

[253]   *Tafsir Al-Jalalayn*, pp. 122-124.

[254]   *Tafsir Ibn 'Abbas*, p. 68.

[255]   *Tafsir Ahsanul-Bayan*, Vol. 1, p. 290.

This permission is for those Muslims who live in a non-Muslim state. If they fear repression, they may profess friendship with the non-Muslims verbally.[256]

So Muslims professing friendship with non-Muslims are not necessarily contravening 5:51 and the many other such verses in the Koran. These Muslims might be following the exception allowed in 3:28, smiling *in the face of some people although our hearts curse them.* Or they simply might not be devout Muslims at the time.

The same principle is applied in 16:106 where Muslims are allowed to deny their faith under duress. Here is that verse:

Chapter 16, Verse 106

> *Whosever disbelieved in Allah after his belief, except him who is forced thereto and whose heart is at rest with Faith; but such as open their breasts to disbelief, on them is wrath from Allah, and theirs will be a great torment.*

Ibn Kathir explained the meaning of this verse in a section titled *Allah's Wrath against the Apostate, except for the One Who is forced into Disbelief:*

> *Allah tells us that He is angry with them who willingly disbelieve in Him after clearly believing in Him, who open their hearts to disbelief finding peace in that, because they understood the faith yet they still turned away from it. They will suffer severe punishment in the Hereafter, because they preferred this life to the Hereafter, and they left the faith for the sake of this world and Allah did not guide their hearts and help them to stand firm in the true religion.*[257]

---

[256]   Ibid.

[257]   *Tafsir Ibn Kathir*, Vol. 5, p. 529.

Ibn Kathir then explained the phrase *except him who is forced thereto*:

> *This is an exception in the case of one who utters*
> *statements of disbelief and verbally agrees with the*
> *Mushrikin* [non-Muslims] *because he is forced to do so by*
> *the beatings and abuse to which he is subjected, but his*
> *heart refuses to accept what he is saying, and he is, in*
> *reality, at peace with his faith in Allah and His*
> *Messenger.*[258]

The *Tafsir Al-Jalalayn* also acknowledged the exception mentioned in this verse, and then pointed out that this verse was "a severe threat" to those who apostatize.[259]

The *Tafsir Ahsanul-Bayan* provided a similar explanation:

> *As Al-Qurtubi said, scholars are unanimous that whoever*
> *renounces the faith under duress to save his life, his heart*
> *content with the faith, he is not to be considered a*
> *disbeliever. The punitive laws relating to heresy...do not*
> *apply to him.*[260]

This modern *tafsir* then explained the phrase *on them is wrath from Allah*:

> *That is the punishment of heresy: Awful doom and the*
> *wrath of Allah. A heretic shall be slain. That is his*
> *temporal punishment...*[261]

Here is the incident that led to this verse being "revealed" to Muhammad:

---

[258]   Ibid., p. 530.

[259]   *Tafsir Al-Jalalayn*, p. 583.

[260]   *Tafsir Ahsanul-Bayan*, Vol. 3, p. 247.

[261]   Ibid.

Said Ibn 'Abbas: "This verse was revealed about 'Ammar ibn Yasir. The idolaters had taken him away along with his father Yasir, his mother Sumayyah...and tortured them. As for Sumayyah, she was tied up between two camels and stabbed with a spear in her female organ. She was told: 'You embraced Islam for the men', and was then killed. Her husband Yasir was also killed. They were the first two persons who were killed in Islam. As for 'Ammar, he was coerced to let them hear what they wanted to hear. The Messenger of Allah, Allah bless him and give him peace, was told that 'Ammar has renounced faith, but he said: 'Never, 'Ammar is filled with faith from his head to his toes; faith is admixed with his flesh and blood!' 'Ammar then went to see the Messenger of Allah, Allah bless him and give him peace, crying. The Messenger of Allah, Allah bless him and give him peace, wiped his tears with his own hand and said: 'if they return to you, let them hear again what you told them.' Then, Allah, exalted is He, revealed this verse."[262]

It is interesting to note that 'Ammar actually did renounce Islam. However, Muhammad forgave him because he had been coerced. But Muhammad also told 'Ammar that even though he had been forgiven and accepted back into the fold of Islam, he could still deceive the idolaters by again denying Islam: "if they return to you, let them hear again what you told them." Muhammad encouraged the deception to continue if necessary.

So we can see that Muslims are allowed to deceive non-Muslims because it is authorized by the Koran and by the teachings of Muhammad; the only requirement is that they stay true to Islam in their hearts.

---

[262]   *Al-Wahidi's Asbab al-Nuzul*, p. 142.

This approach to deception was expanded upon and formalized by the utilitarian comments of the noted Islamic scholar, Imam Abu Hamid Ghazali (1058-1111 AD):

> *Speaking is a means to achieve objectives. If a praiseworthy aim is attainable through both telling the truth and lying, it is unlawful to accomplish through lying because there is no need for it. When it is possible to achieve such an aim by lying but not by telling the truth, it is permissible to lie if attaining the goal is permissible, and obligatory to lie if the goal is obligatory....Whether the purpose is war, settling a disagreement, or gaining the sympathy of a victim legally entitled to retaliate against one so that he will forbear to do so; it is not unlawful to lie when any of these aims can only be attained through lying. But it is religiously more precautionary in all such cases to employ words that give a misleading impression, meaning to intend by one's words something that is literally true, in respect to which one is not lying, while the outward purport of the words deceives the hearer, though even if one does not have such an intention and merely lies without intending anything else, it is not unlawful in the above circumstances...One should compare the bad consequences entailed by lying to those entailed by telling the truth, and if the consequences of telling the truth are more damaging, one is entitled to lie, though if the reverse is true or if one does not know which entails more damage, then lying is unlawful...Strictness is to forgo lying in every case where it is not legally obligatory.*[263]

---

[263]   *Reliance of the Traveller*, r8.2, pp. 745-746.

Appendix 1: Glossary & Important Concepts

Abrogation
If there is a conflict between the messages of two verses in the Koran, then the most recently "revealed" verse is the one to be followed. See "Important Concepts," No. 2, for more information.

Allah
The god of Islam.

Allahu Akbar
Allah, the god of Islam, is greatest and above all others.

Apostasy
Leaving Islam for another religion. Muhammad said that anyone doing so should be killed.

Dhimmi (dimmy)
A non-Muslim living under the protection of an Islamic government. Also see Jizya.

Ghazwah
A military expedition personally led by Muhammad.

Hadith (hahdeeth)
A story related by a companion of Muhammad about a teaching, example, or statement of Muhammad they had personally seen or heard.

Hajj
Pilgrimage to Mecca that is obligatory on each Muslim once in their lifetime if they are able.

Hijrah
The emigration in 622 AD of Muhammad and his small band of Muslims from Mecca to Medina. This marked the beginning of the Islamic calendar.

Imam (eemahm)
Leading scholar, prayer leader, leader in a Muslim community.

Iman (eemahn)
Sincere and unconditional faith/belief in Islam

Islam
The word means "submission."

Jizya
Head tax imposed on all non-Muslims living under the protection of an Islamic government.

Koran
The sacred book of Islam. It consists of timeless, infallible "revelations" Muhammad received from Allah and dictated to his followers. The Koran was compiled as a book after Muhammad's death.

Muhammad
The prophet of Islam who received "revelations" from Allah. Also known as Allah's Apostle and the Messenger of Allah. He lived from 570-632.

Mujahideen
Fighters for the Cause of Allah

Mushrikun
Polytheists, pagans, idolaters and disbelievers in the Oneness of Allah and His Messenger Muhammad; people who associate partners/a Son with Allah.

Muslim
A person who submits; a follower of the religion of Islam.

People of the Book/Scripture
Jews and Christians

Sharia Law
Islamic sacred law based predominantly on the Koran and the Sunnah.

Shia (sheeah)
The second largest sect in Islam, consisting of 10-13% of the Muslims in the world. Concentrated largely in Iran.

Sira (seerah)
The Life of Muhammad (Sirat Rasul Allah), the authoritative biography of Muhammad written by Ibn Ishaq after Muhammad's death.

Sunnah (soonah)
The Way of Muhammad, consisting of the examples, ways, and teachings of Muhammad that have become rules to be followed by Muslims. The Sunnah is based on the information found in the Sira and the authoritative hadith collections.

Sunni (soonee)
The major sect in Islam, consisting of 80-85% of the Muslims in the world.

Taqiyya (tahkeeya)
Deception directed at non-Muslims. This is specifically authorized in two verses of the Koran: 3:28 and 16:106.

Important Concepts

1.   **"But it's not in the Koran"** - This implies that if it is not mentioned in the Koran, then it is not a part of Islam. The reality is that the information in the *Sira* and the authoritative *hadith* collections is second only to the Koran in understanding, and being a part of, Islam. The *Sira* and *hadiths* provide the vast majority of what is known about Muhammad and his teachings, and authoritative *hadiths* were used by Islamic scholars to explain the meaning of verses in the Koran.

2.   **"But what about the peaceful verses in the Koran?"** - It depends. Are they verses from Mecca or verses from Medina? The verses of the Koran were "revealed" to Muhammad over a period of about 23 years, beginning in 610 while he was in Mecca. He continued to receive "revelations" after he left Mecca and emigrated with some of his followers to Medina in 622. While in Mecca, Muhammad was just starting the religion of Islam, and it was not generally well received. Perhaps as a

145

result of this resistance, the Koranic verses "revealed" in Mecca were generally more peaceful and accommodating toward non-Muslims than the verses later "revealed" in Medina. The verses "revealed" in Medina had a general tendency to be less tolerant, more belligerent, and more inclined to make sharp differentiations between Muslims (believers) and non-Muslims (disbelievers). This led to conflicts between the message of a Meccan verse and that of a Medinan verse addressing the same general topic. But how can there be such a conflict if the Koran is the timeless, infallible, "revealed" word of Allah? This was covered in a Medinan verse that introduced the concept of "abrogation":

> *Whatever a Verse (revelation) do We abrogate or cause to be forgotten, We bring a better one or similar to it. Know you not that Allah is Able to do all things?*

Koran, Chapter 2, Verse 106

Abrogation means that if there is a conflict between the messages of two "revelations" in the Koran, then the most recent "revelation" is the one to be followed. Consequently, a "revelation" made in Medina would supersede a similar, earlier "revelation" made in Mecca if there was a conflict between the two.

3.   **Dying for raisins? Or, is there anything in the Koran that promises 72 virgins for a holy martyr?**

> *I don't see any of it is in the Koran for the pledge of 72 virgins. This notion of 72 virgins actually comes from a mistranslation, uh, with the real translation being 72 raisins.*

> *Irshad Manji, Director Moral Courage Project, New York University, in the ABC 20/20 Special - Islam: Questions and Answers (October 1, 2010)*

146

Irshad Manji is partially correct; the statement about "72 virgins" is not in the Koran. But the notion is not the result of a "mistranslation." It is in one of the authoritative *hadith* collections:

> *Al-Miqdam bin Ma'diykarib narrated that the Messenger of Allah said: "There are six things with Allah for the martyr: He is forgiven with the first flow of blood (he suffers), he is shown his place in Paradise, he is protected from punishment in the grave, secured from the greatest terror, the crown of dignity is placed upon his head - and its gems are better than the world and what is in it - he is married to seventy-two wives among Al-Huril-'Ayn of Paradise, and he may intercede for seventy of his close relatives."*

Jami' At-Tirmidhi, Vol. 3, No. 1663, p. 410

The *Al-Huril-'Ayn* (*Houris, Hur*) are the very fair female virgins of Paradise.

However, there was another *hadith* that gave a different breakdown on the nature of the "72 virgins":

> *It was narrated from Abu Umamah that the Messenger of Allah said: "There is no one whom Allah will admit to Paradise but Allah will marry him to seventy-two wives, two from houris and seventy from his inheritance from the people of Hell, all of whom will have desirable front passages and he will have a male member that never becomes flaccid..." Hisham bin Khalid said: "From his inheritance from the people of Hell" means: "Men who enter Hell, and the people of Paradise will inherit their wives, just as the wife of Pharaoh will be inherited."*

Sunan Ibn Majah, Vol. 5, No. 4337, pp. 423-424

Irshad Manji or the Messenger of Allah? This is a perfect example of the pitfalls of listening to personal perspectives on Islam.

Appendix 2: HSM Transcript

Transcript: Speech of HSM Leader, Shaykh Mukhtar Abu Zubayr, regarding the #Westgate Operation

Voice of GobIslam

All praise is due to Almighty Allah, the Lord of the worlds, and victory is for the Muttaqeen (the pious believers) and there is no animosity except against the oppressors, and may peace and blessings be upon the noblest of Prophets and Messengers. As for what follows:

Allah, the Exalted, said:

> *"And when they advanced to meet Jalut (Goliath) and his forces, they invoked: "Our Lord! Pour forth on us*

*patience, and make our feet firm and make us victorious
over the disbelieving people.*

*So they routed them by Allah's Leave and Dawud (David)
killed Jalut (Goliath), and Allah gave him [Dawud
(David)] the kingdom and Al-Hikmah (Prophethood), and
taught him of that which He willed. And if Allah did not
check one set of people by means of another, the earth
would indeed be full of mischief. But Allah is full of bounty
to the 'Alamin (mankind, jinn and all that exists)*

And the Messenger of Allah, may peace and blessing be upon him, said:

*"I have been sent ahead of the Hour with the sword so
that Allaah will be worshipped alone without partners,
and my provision has been placed under the shade of my
spear, and humiliation has been decreed for those who go
against my command"*

*On Saturday 21 September 2013, and which was just 10 days after the
anniversary date of the blessed 911 operations, a battle which is among
the epic battles in the history of Islam began in Nairobi, and in which
some of the Mujahideen Martyrom [sic] Seekers have written with their
blood. Allah has honoured the Mujahideen fighters to write this epic battle
– the Badar of Nairobi – with their blood and to change the course of
history and avenge the deaths of the weak, oppressed Muslims.*

*The Mujahideen fighters refused to accept the invasion of their Muslim
lands and the massacre of innocent Muslims and live with such
humiliation. They could not accept the persistent theft of their land's
resources which the Kenyan leaders and Western companies have
conspired to plunder.*

*The Mujahideen fought against the oppression of their brothers in prisons
of the Crusaders and their apostate allies, delivering a message that said:
"as long as our brothers are being oppressed in prisons, peace will never
come to the oppressors who are holding them."*

149

So, we say to them, congratulations and we give them glad tiding of the prophet's words, may peace and blessings be upon him, when he was asked:

> *"Which of the martyrs is best? He said: "Those who, when they take up their position in the ranks for battle, do not turn their faces away until they are killed. They will be in the highest dwellings in Paradise, and their Lord smiles upon them, and when your Lord smiles upon a slave in this world, he will not be brought to account."*

In another narration, when the Prophet, peace be upon him, was asked:

> *"What type of jihad is best? He said: "The one whose horse is killed and whose blood is shed."*

So congratulations! You have renewed the fact that the Mujahideen's objective of Jihad is deposing the apostate tyrants, supporting the weak and standing in the face of oppression. You have manifestly proven how valuable the blood of the Muslim is and how the Mujahideen take great measures to safeguard the inviolable blood of the Muslims.

Many lessons can be derived from this epic battle 'Badar of Nairobi'. The battle is a testament to the power of Eeman [faith] and clearly illustrates that nothing can stand against it.

Allah, the Exalted, says:

> *"You killed them not, but Allah killed them. And you (Muhammad) threw not when you did throw, but Allah threw, that He might test the believers by a fair trial from Him. Verily, Allah is All-Hearer, All-Knower.*
>
> *This (is the fact) and surely, Allah weakens the deceitful plots of the disbelievers."*
> *[Anfal, 17-18]*

The attack at Westgate Mall was to torment the Kenyan leaders who've impulsively invaded the Islamic Wilaayat [state, lands]. It was also a retribution against the Western states that supported the Kenyan invasion and are spilling the blood of innocent Muslims in order to pave the way for their mineral companies. It also acts as a clear testament to the historical blunder that the Kenyan government made when it decided to invade the Islamic Wilaayaat.

The attack has also glaringly illuminated the sheer vulnerability of the different sections of the Kenyan forces, be they police, intelligence or the military, and this was demonstrated by the utter failure that their forces came against when they tried to storm the building that was occupied by the Mujahideen.

Allah, the Exalted, says:

> *"The likeness of those who take (false deities as) Auliya' (protectors, helpers) other than Allah is the likeness of a spider who builds (for itself) a house; but verily, the frailest (weakest) of houses is the spider's house – if they but knew." [Ankaboot, 41]*

The attack is also a slap in the face of on the dwindling economy of the Kenyan government and has also successfully foiled the clandestine schemes of the Zionist Jews in Kenya. It's a disaster for the Western politicians and their intelligence apparatuse [sic] who have miserably failed to save their own citizens.

We tell the Kenyan public: You have entered into a war that is not yours and is serving against your national interests. You have voluntarily given up on your security and economy and lost many of your sons. You are taking an active part in the massacres that are being perpetrated by your military in Kismayo and the neighboring regions. That is so because it's you who have chosen your politicians, the taxes that you pay are being

151

used to arm Uhuru Kenyatta's army that is actively killing Muslims and it's you who have supported your government's decision to go to war.[264]

Allah, the Exalted, says:

> *"And those who disbelieve say: "We believe not in this Qur'an nor in that which was before it." But if you could see when the Thalimun (polytheists and wrong-doers) will be made to stand before their Lord, how they will cast the (blaming) word one to another! Those who were deemed weak will say to those who were arrogant: "Had it not been for you, we should certainly have been believers!*

> *And those who were arrogant will say to those who were deemed weak: "Did we keep you back from guidance after it had come to you? Nay, but you were Mujrimin (polytheists, sinners, disbelievers, criminals).*

> *Those who were deemed weak will say to those who were arrogant: "Nay, but it was your plotting by night and day: when you ordered us to disbelieve in Allah and set up rivals to Him!" And each of them (parties) will conceal their own regrets (for disobeying Allah during this worldly life), when they behold the torment. And We shall put iron collars round the necks of those who disbelieved. Are they requited aught except what they used to do?" [Saba, 31-34]*

Now, you still have an opportunity to reflect and reach a conclusive decision and hold your politicians to account. Do not wait for Uhuru kenyatta [sic] to bring about a solution to your problems as he has no further objectives beyond that presidential seat. It was he who spilt the blood of thousands of ordinary Kenyans during the previous elections and is today prepared for thousands more of your sons to die inside their

---

264   Uhuru Kenyatta was sworn in as the president of Kenya on April 9, 2013.

country as well as abroad in order for him to prolong his stay in power, please his Western masters and accomplish their objectives. Do not be misled by the International Criminal Court as it's simply a facade to create further publicity for Uhuru.

There is no way that you, the Kenyan public, could possibly endure a prolonged war in Somalia and you cannot also withstand a war of attrition inside your own country. So make your choice today and withdraw all your forces from the Islamic Wilaayaat, otherwise be prepared for an abundance of blood that will be spilt in your country, economic downfall and displacement.

Allah, the Exalted, says:

> *"Fight against them so that Allah will punish them by your hands and disgrace them and give you victory over them and heal the breasts of a believing people*
>
> *And remove the anger of their (believers') hearts. Allah accepts the repentance of whom He wills. Allah is All-Knowing, All-Wise." [At-Tawbah, 14-15]*

And the last of our call is that all praise is due to Allah, the Lord of the Worlds.[265]

---

[265]   Speech accessed on October 1, 2013 at:

http://somalimidnimo.com/salafi/2013/09/transcript-speech-of-hsm-leader-shaykh-mukhtar-abu-zubayr-regarding-the-westgate-operation/.

Appendix 3: Killing According to Muhammad

KILLING ACCORDING TO MUHAMMAD

YEAR	PERMISSIBLE			NOT PERMISSIBLE	
	NO COMMENTS FROM MUHAMMAD	NON-COMBATANTS OR OTHERS	CHILDREN/WOMEN	NON-COMBATANTS OR OTHERS	CHILDREN/WOMEN
623	EXPEDITION OF HAMZA B. 'ABD AL-MUTTALIB EXPEDITION TO RABIGH EXPEDITION TO AL-KHARRAR GHAZWAH OF AL-ABWA GHAZWAH OF BUWAT GHAZWAH OF THE FIRST BADR GHAZWAH OF DHU L-'USHAYRA EXPEDITION TO NAKHLA **				
624		**KILLING OF ABU 'AFAK** Muhammad sent a Muslim to kill a 120 year old man. Muhammad said, *Who will deal with this rascal for me?*	**KILLING OF 'ASMA BT. MARWAN** Muhammad sent a Muslim to kill a poetess who had insulted him & vilified Islam. Muhammad said, *Who will rid me of Marwan's daughter?*	**BATTLE OF BADR** Muhammad forbad the killing of certain warriors among the Quraysh.	

** - Surprise Attack by the Muslims

1

		PERMISSIBLE		NOT PERMISSIBLE	
YEAR	NO COMMENTS FROM MUHAMMAD	NON-COMBATANTS OR OTHERS	CHILDREN/WOMEN	NON-COMBATANTS OR OTHERS	CHILDREN/WOMEN
624 (cont)					
	GHAZWAH OF THE BANI QAYNUQA				
	EXPEDITION AGAINST THE BANI SULAYM				
	GHAZWAH OF AL-SAWIQ				
	GHAZWAH OF QARARA AL-KUDR	KILLING OF KA'B B. AL-ASHRAF Muhammad sent some Muslims to kill a Jewish poet who had criticized him. Muhammad said, *Who will kill Ka'b bin Al-Ashraf who has hurt Allah and his Messenger?* The next morning, after Ka'b had been killed, Muhammad said, *Whoever of the Jews falls into your hands, kill him.*			
	GHAZWAH OF DHU AMARR				
	GHAZWAH AGAINST THE BANI SULAYM				
	EXPEDITION TO AL-QARADA **				
625	BATTLE OF UHUD The Quraysh attacked Medina bringing some of their women along to encourage them. Muhammad was advised of the women but said nothing.				

** - Surprise Attack by the Muslims

2

155

		PERMISSIBLE		NOT PERMISSIBLE	
YEAR	NO COMMENTS FROM MUHAMMAD	NON-COMBATANTS OR OTHERS	CHILDREN/WOMEN	NON-COMBATANTS OR OTHERS	CHILDREN/WOMEN
625 (cont)					
	GHAZWAH OF HAMRA' AL-ASAD				
	EXPEDITION TO QATAN				
	EXPEDITION TO BI'R MA'UNAH				
	EXPEDITION OF AL-RAJI				
		EXPEDITION TO KILL A QURAYSH LEADER Muhammad sent two Muslims to Mecca to kill Abu Sufyan. Muhammad ordered, *Go to Abu Sufyan b. Harb and kill him.* The two Muslims were not successful.			
	GHAZWAH AGAINST THE BANI NADIR				
	GHAZWAH OF DHAT AL-RIQA' Muhammad led a force against some Arab tribes. There was no battle, but the wife of a non-Muslim was somehow killed.				
626					
	GHAZWAH OF BADER AL-MAW'ID				
	GHAZWAH OF DUMAT AL-JANDAL				

** - Surprise Attack by the Muslims

3

YEAR	PERMISSIBLE			NOT PERMISSIBLE	
	NO COMMENTS FROM MUHAMMAD	NON-COMBATANTS OR OTHERS	CHILDREN/WOMEN	NON-COMBATANTS OR OTHERS	CHILDREN/WOMEN
627	BATTLE OF THE TRENCH		**GHAZWAH AGAINST THE BANI QURAYZAH** After this Jewish tribe surrendered, Muhammad supervised the beheading of all the males in the tribe who had reached puberty, whether they had fought or not (total of 600-900 males). One woman was beheaded for having killed a Muslim by dropping a millstone on his head.		**THE KILLING OF ABU RAFI'** Abu Rafi' had criticized Muhammad. He ordered five Muslims to kill Abu Rafi'. Muhammad told them not to kill women or children.
		THE KILLING OF SUFYAN B. KHALID Muhammad sent a Muslim to kill Sufyan because he was gathering tribes against the Muslims. Sufyan was killed inside his tent, *leaving his women crying over him.*			
	EXPEDITION TO AL-QURTA' *GHAZWAH* AGAINST THE BANI LIHYAN				

** - Surprise Attack by the Muslims

4

157

	PERMISSIBLE			NOT PERMISSIBLE	
YEAR	NO COMMENTS FROM MUHAMMAD	NON-COMBATANTS OR OTHERS	CHILDREN/WOMEN	NON-COMBATANTS OR OTHERS	CHILDREN/WOMEN
627 (cont)	GHAZWAH TO DHU QARAD				EXPEDITION TO DUMAT AL-JANDAL
	EXPEDITION TO AL-GHAMR				Muhammad sent a raiding party to "invite" this tribe to Islam. He told his warriors not to kill "a boy" or "children." The tribe accepted Islam.
	EXPEDITION TO DHU AL-QASSAH				
	2nd EXPEDITION TO DHU AL-QASSAH **				
	EXPEDITION TO AL-JAMUM				
	EXPEDITION TO AL-'EIS **				
	EXPEDITION TO AL-TARAF				
	EXPEDITION TO HISMA				
	EXPEDITION TO WADI AL-QURA				
			GHAZWAH TO AL-MURAYSI' (BANI AL-MUSTALIQ) ** Muhammad led a Muslim force against the Bani Al-Mustaliq tribe. After facing resistance from the tribe, Muhammad commanded that the tribe's fortifications be set on fire, even though the Muslims knew there were women and children inside the fortifications. The Bani Al-Mustaliq were defeated and their women and children were divided among the Muslims.		
	EXPEDITION TO MADYAN				
	EXPEDITION TO FADAK				

** - Surprise Attack by the Muslims

	PERMISSIBLE			NOT PERMISSIBLE	
YEAR	NO COMMENTS FROM MUHAMMAD	NON-COMBATANTS OR OTHERS	CHILDREN/WOMEN	NON-COMBATANTS OR OTHERS	CHILDREN/WOMEN
628	**2nd EXPEDITION TO WADI AL-QURA** Muhammad sent a raiding party. Among the captives was an old lady who was then cruelly killed. **EXPEDITION TO USAYR B. ZARIM** **EXPEDITION TO AL-'URANIYYIN**		**TREATY OF AL-HUDAYBIYAH** Muhammad was asked if it was allowed to kill the women and children of the enemy during a night attack. Muhammad approved, saying, *They are from them.* When the Muslims found out that the forces opposing them had brought their women and children, Muhammad asked his warriors, *Do you recommend that I should destroy the families and offspring of those who want to stop us...?* The Muslims decided against this and signed a treaty. **GHAZWAH TO KHAYBAR** Muhammad led a Muslim army against the Jewish community of Khaybar. Khaybar consisted of multiple fortifications. After conquering some of the fortifications, the Muslims found catapults, which they then used to hurl stones against the other fortresses. The Muslims knew women and children were in these fortresses.		

** - Surprise Attack by the Muslims

159

	PERMISSIBLE			NOT PERMISSIBLE	
YEAR	NO COMMENTS FROM MUHAMMAD	NON-COMBATANTS OR OTHERS	CHILDREN/WOMEN	NON-COMBATANTS OR OTHERS	CHILDREN/WOMEN
628 (cont)	3rd EXPEDITION TO WADI AL-QURA				
	EXPEDITION TO TURBA				
			**EXPEDITION OF ABU BAKR TO NAJD ** ** Muhammad sent a raiding party to Najd. One of the Muslim warriors later said, *We attacked at dawn, raiding the people of the oasis, and killed them, nine or seven households*. He stated, *I slew with my hand members of seven families of the polytheists*. Abu Bakr led the raiding party.		
	EXPEDITION TO FADAK				
629	EXPEDITION TO AL-MAYFA'A				
	EXPEDITION TO AL-JINAB				
	EXPEDITION AGAINST THE BANI SULAYM				
	EXPEDITION TO AL-KADAYD **				
	EXPEDITION AGAINST BANI 'AMIR				
	EXPEDITION TO DHAT ATLAH				
	EXPEDITION TO DHAT AL-SALASIL				
	EXPEDITION TO AL-KHABAT				
	EXPEDITION TO AL-GHABAH **				**EXPEDITION TO MUTA** Muhammad sent 3,000 warriors to Mu'ta. He ordered them not to kill women and children.

** - Surprise Attack by the Muslims

160

		PERMISSIBLE		NOT PERMISSIBLE	
YEAR	NO COMMENTS FROM MUHAMMAD	NON-COMBATANTS OR OTHERS	CHILDREN/WOMEN	NON-COMBATANTS OR OTHERS	CHILDREN/WOMEN
629 (cont)	EXPEDITION AGAINST IDAM				**EXPEDITION TO KHADIRA** Muhammad orderd his warriors not to kill women and children.
630			**CONQUEST OF MECCA** Muhammad marched on Mecca with 10,000 Muslim warriors. He ordered the killing of some specific men and women. After Mecca was conquered, some of those specified to be killed converted to Islam and were spared. Others were killed. **EXPEDITION IN THE DIRECTION OF YALAMLAM** Muhammad sent out a force of 200 warriors to attack those who were not following Islam. **EXPEDITION IN THE DIRECTION OF 'URANA** Muhammad sent out a force of 300 warriors to attack those who were not following Islam. **EXPEDITION AGAINST AL-'UZZA** Muhammad sent Khalid b. al-Walid with 30 warriors to destroy the statue of the pagan goddess Al-'Uzza. Al-Walid did so. A black woman appeared and he killed her with his sword. Muhammad said she was Al-'Uzza.		

** - Surprise Attack by the Muslims

	PERMISSIBLE			NOT PERMISSIBLE	
YEAR	NO COMMENTS FROM MUHAMMAD	NON-COMBATANTS OR OTHERS	CHILDREN/WOMEN	NON-COMBATANTS OR OTHERS	CHILDREN/WOMEN
630 (cont)	**EXPEDITION AGAINST MANAT** Muhammad sent a force of 20 warriors to destroy the statue of the pagan goddess Manat. They destroyed the statue and their leader killed a black woman who appeared.		**EXPEDITION AGAINST THE BANI JADHIMA** Muhammad sent 350 Muslim warriors out with the command, *Slay the people as long as you do not hear a mu'adhdhin* [one who calls Muslims to prayer] *or see a mosque*. The Bani Jadhima laid down their weapons claiming to already be Muslims. Nevertheless, their warriors were bound and many were beheaded. One of the women kissed the head of one of the warriors until she was also killed.		*GHAZWAH* AGAINST HUNAYN Muhammad led a force of 12,000 Muslim warriors against two Arab tribes in the valley of Hunayn. Muhammad was advised there were woman and and children with the tribes. He said, *That will be the plunder of the Muslims tomorrow, God willing!* During the battle Muslims started killing some of the children. Muhammad stopped them from killing the children. After the battle he came upon a dead woman. He forbad the killing of women, children, laborers, and hired slaves.
	EXPEDITION TO AWTAS				

** - Surprise Attack by the Muslims

9

YEAR	PERMISSIBLE			NOT PERMISSIBLE	
	NO COMMENTS FROM MUHAMMAD	NON-COMBATANTS OR OTHERS	CHILDREN/WOMEN	NON-COMBATANTS OR OTHERS	CHILDREN/WOMEN
630 (cont)			*GHAZWAH AGAINST TA'IF* — Muhammad led the Muslims to besiege the fortress at Al-Ta'if. The siege lasted 14-19 days, and catapults were used to throw stones at the fortress. Muhammad knew that women and children were inside the fortress.		
	EXPEDITION AGAINST THE BANU TAMIM				
	EXPEDITION TO KHATH'AM **				
	EXPEDITION AGAINST THE BANU KILAB				
	EXPEDITION TO HABASHA				
	EXPEDITION TO AL-FULS **				
	EXPEDITION AGAINST AL-JINAB				
			GHAZWAH OF TABUK — There were some Muslims who were encouraging others not to go on this *Ghazwah*. When Muhammad learned that they were meeting in the house of a Jew, Muhammad ordered that the house be burned down on them.		
	EXPEDITION AGAINST AL-UKAYDIR **				
631	EXPEDITION TO THE BANI AL-HARITH		10		

** - Surprise Attack by the Muslims

163

YEAR	PERMISSIBLE			NOT PERMISSIBLE	
	NO COMMENTS FROM MUHAMMAD	NON-COMBATANTS OR OTHERS	CHILDREN/WOMEN	NON-COMBATANTS OR OTHERS	CHILDREN/WOMEN
631 (cont)	EXPEDITION TO YEMEN EXPEDITION TO JURASH				

EXPEDITION TO DHUL-KHALAS

Muhammad sent 150 Muslim warriors to destroy the pagan shrine of Dhul-Khalas. They destroyed the shrine *and killed whoever was present there*. Muhammad *invoked good* upon the Muslim warriors.

632

THE EXPEDITION TO MUTA **

Shortly before he died, Muhammad ordered a surprise attack on the town of Ubna. He said, *Do not kill a new born or a woman...* But it was also reported that Muhammad ordered the commander, *Attack the people of Ubna early in the morning and set fire (to their camp)*, and *to destroy and burn*. A Muslim historian wrote about the attack: *He killed him who met him, enslaved him whom he could, set fire to their boats, and burnt their dwellings, farms and palm-groves which turned into whirl-wind* [sic] *of smoke.*

11

** - Surprise Attack by the Muslims

164

Appendix 4: Killing According to Muhammad (Summary)

KILLING ACCORDING TO MUHAMMAD - SUMMARY

YEAR	NO COMMENTS FROM MUHAMMAD	PERMISSIBLE		NOT PERMISSIBLE	
		NON-COMBATANTS OR OTHERS	CHILDREN/WOMEN	NON-COMBATANTS OR OTHERS	CHILDREN/WOMEN
623	4 EXPEDITIONS 4 GHAZWAHS				
624	1 EXPEDITION 3 GHAZWAHS	KILLING OF ABU 'AFAK	KILLING OF 'ASMA BT. MARWAN	BATTLE OF BADR	
	1 EXPEDITION 2 GHAZWAHS	KILLING OF KA'B B. AL-ASHRAF			
625	BATTLE OF UHUD 3 EXPEDITIONS 1 GHAZWAH	EXPEDITION TO KILL A QURAYSH LEADER			
	1 GHAZWAH GHAZWAH OF DHAT AL-RIQA'				
626	2 GHAZWAHS				

1

165

YEAR	NO COMMENTS FROM MUHAMMAD	PERMISSIBLE		NOT PERMISSIBLE	
		NON-COMBATANTS OR OTHERS	CHILDREN/WOMEN	NON-COMBATANTS OR OTHERS	CHILDREN/WOMEN
627	BATTLE OF THE TRENCH				
		GHAZWAH AGAINST THE BANI QURAYZAH			
					THE KILLING OF ABU RAFI'
		THE KILLING OF SUFYAN B. KHALID			
	9 EXPEDITIONS				
	2 GHAZWAHS				
		GHAZWAH TO AL-MURAYSI' (BANI AL-MUSTALIQ)			
	2 EXPEDITIONS				EXPEDITION TO DUMAT AL-JANDAL
628	2nd EXPEDITION TO WADI AL-QURA				
	2 EXPEDITIONS		TREATY OF AL-HUDAYBIYAH		
			GHAZWAH TO KHAYBAR		
	2 EXPEDITIONS	EXPEDITION OF ABU BAKR TO NAJD			
	1 EXPEDITION				
629	6 EXPEDITIONS				EXPEDITION TO MUTA
	3 EXPEDITIONS				EXPEDITION TO KHADIRA
	1 EXPEDITION				

2

166

	PERMISSIBLE			NOT PERMISSIBLE	
YEAR	NO COMMENTS FROM MUHAMMAD	NON-COMBATANTS OR OTHERS	CHILDREN/WOMEN	NON-COMBATANTS OR OTHERS	CHILDREN/WOMEN
630			CONQUEST OF MECCA		
			EXPEDITION IN THE DIRECTION OF YALAMLAM		
			EXPEDITION IN THE DIRECTION OF 'URANA		
			EXPEDITION AGAINST AL-'UZZA		
	EXPEDITION AGAINST MANAT		EXPEDITION AGAINST THE BANI JADHIMA		GHAZWAH AGAINST HUNAYN
	1 EXPEDITION		GHAZWAH AGAINST TA'IF		
	6 EXPEDITIONS		GHAZWAH OF TABUK		
	1 EXPEDITION				
631	3 EXPEDITIONS		EXPEDITION TO DHUL-KHALAS		
632				THE EXPEDITION TO MUTA	

3

Appendix 5: The First Country to Recognize the U.S.

I also know that Islam has always been a part of America's story. The first nation to recognize my country was Morocco. In signing the Treaty of Tripoli in 1796, our second President, John Adams, wrote, "The United States has in itself no character of enmity against the laws, religion or tranquility of Muslims."

President Barack Hussein Obama, June 4, 2009,
during his speech in Cairo, Egypt[266]

---

[266]   The actual name of the 1796 Treaty of Tripoli was the *Treaty of Peace and Friendship between the United States of America and the Bey and Subjects of Tripoli of Barbary*. It can be found online at The Avalon Project – Documents in Law, History and Diplomacy, Yale Law School, at:

http://avalon.law.yale.edu/18th_century/bar1796t.asp.

Obama's mention of the 1796 Treaty of Tripoli was curious. Upon hearing his statement about the recognition of the United States by Morocco, followed by the mention of the Treaty of Tripoli, one could have the impression that the treaty between the United States and Morocco was called the Treaty of Tripoli. However, the 1796 Treaty of Tripoli was actually a separate treaty between a young, somewhat weak United States and the Muslim Bey of Tripoli, a branch of the Barbary Pirates that was raiding American ships and enslaving American sailors.

This Treaty of Tripoli was in reality a treaty in which the young United States agreed to pay tribute to the Bey so that he would quit attacking American ships! Article 10 of this treaty stated:

> *The money and presents **demanded** [my emphasis] by the Bey of Tripoli as a full and satisfactory consideration on his part and on the part of his subjects for this treaty of perpetual peace and friendship are acknowledged to have been recieved [sic] by him…*

168

As President Obama's statement shows, it is not at all unusual to hear the claim that the Muslim country of Morocco was the first country to recognize the young United States. But this claim is simply wrong. France was the first country to officially recognize and have diplomatic relations with the young United States.

Let's start out by learning about the early history of relations between the United States and Morocco. The following is a detailed history from the website of the United States Embassy in Morocco; it is lengthy, provides the essential facts about this matter, and, although it is the official view of the United States government, it was apparently never read by President Obama or his speech writers.[267]

U.S. Morocco Relations - The Beginning

Morocco and the United States have a long history of friendly relations. This North African nation was one of the first states to seek diplomatic relations with America. In 1777, Sultan Sidi Muhammad Ben Abdullah, the most progressive of the Barbary leaders who ruled Morocco from 1757 to 1790, announced his desire for friendship with the United States. The Sultan's overture was part of a new policy he was implementing as a result of his recognition of the need to establish peaceful relations with the Christian powers and his desire to establish

---

Among the American tribute the Bey had received was forty thousand Spanish dollars, gold and silver watches, and diamond rings. The arrival of the American consul in Tripoli was to bring more tribute payments that included an additional twelve thousand Spanish dollars.

So in a matter of two sentences in his Cairo speech Obama had managed to appeal to his Muslim audience by not only inaccurately presenting history, but by also reminding them about a treaty of submission between a young, weaker United States and a stronger Muslim ruler.

[267]   Accessed on August 9, 2013 at http://morocco.usembassy.gov/early.html.

trade as a basic source of revenue. Faced with serious economic and political difficulties, he was searching for a new method of governing which required changes in his economy. Instead of relying on a standing professional army to collect taxes and enforce his authority, he wanted to establish state-controlled maritime trade as a new, more reliable, and regular source of income which would free him from dependency on the services of the standing army. The opening of his ports to America and other states was part of that new policy.

The Sultan issued a declaration on December 20, 1777, announcing that all vessels sailing under the American flag could freely enter Moroccan ports. The Sultan stated that orders had been given to his corsairs to let the ship "des Americains" and those of other European states with which Morocco had no treaties - Russia Malta, Sardinia, Prussia, Naples, Hungary, Leghorn, Genoa, and Germany - pass freely into Moroccan ports. There they could "take refreshments" and provisions and enjoy the same privileges as other nations that had treaties with Morocco. This action, under the diplomatic practice of Morocco at the end of the 18th century, put the United States on an equal footing with all other nations with which the Sultan had treaties. By issuing this declaration, Morocco became one of the first states to acknowledge publicly the independence of the American Republic.[268]

On February 20, 1778, the sultan of Morocco reissued his December 20, 1777, declaration.[269] American officials,

---

268   So here it is plainly stated that Morocco was merely "one of the first states" to publically "acknowledge" the independence of the United States. This is a far cry from supposedly being the first country to officially recognize the United States.

269   However, on February 6, 1778, France had formally recognized the United States with the Treaty of Alliance, and the Treaty of Amity and Commerce between the United States and France.

however, only belatedly learned of the Sultan's full intentions. Nearly identical to the first, the February 20 declaration was again sent to all consuls and merchants in the ports of Tangier, Sale, and Mogador informing them the Sultan had opened his ports to Americans and nine other European States. Information about the Sultan's desire for friendly relations with the United States first reached Benjamin Franklin, one of the American commissioners in Paris, sometime in late April or early May 1778 from Etienne d'Audibert Caille, a French merchant of Sale. Appointed by the Sultan to serve as Consul for all the nations unrepresented in Morocco, Caille wrote on behalf of the Sultan to Franklin from Cadiz on April 14, 1778, offering to negotiate a treaty between Morocco and the United States on the same terms the Sultan had negotiated with other powers. When he did not receive a reply, Caille wrote Franklin a second letter sometime later that year or in early 1779. When Franklin wrote to the committee on Foreign Affairs in May 1779, he reported he had received two letters from a Frenchman who "offered to act as our Minister with the Emperor" and informed the American commissioner that "His Imperial Majesty wondered why we had never sent to thank him for being the first power on this side of the Atlantic that had acknowledged our independence and opened his ports to us." Franklin, who did not mention the dates of Caille's letters or when he had received them, added that he had ignored these letters because the French advised him that Caille was reputed to be untrustworthy. Franklin stated that the French King was willing to use his good offices with the Sultan whenever Congress desired a treaty and concluded, "whenever a treaty with the Emperor is intended, I suppose some of our naval stores will be an acceptable present and the expectation of continued supplies of such stores a powerful motive for entering into and continuing a friendship."

Since the Sultan received no acknowledgement of his good will gestures by the fall of 1779, he made another attempt to contact the new American government. Under instructions from the Moroccan ruler, Caille wrote a letter to Congress in September

171

1779 in care of Franklin in Paris to announce his appointment as Consul and the Sultan's desire to be at peace with the United States. The Sultan, he reiterated, wished to conclude a treaty "similar to those Which the principal maritime powers have with him." Americans were invited to "come and traffic freely in these ports in like manner as they formerly did under the English flag." Caille also wrote to John Jay, the American representative at Madrid, on April 21, 1780, asking for help in conveying the Sultan's message to Congress and enclosing a copy of Caille's commission from the Sultan to act as Consul for all nations that had none in Morocco, as well as a copy of the February 20, 1778, declaration. Jay received that letter with enclosures in May 1780, but because it was not deemed to be of great importance, he did not forward it and its enclosures to Congress until November 30, 1780.

Before Jay's letter with the enclosures from Caille reached Congress, Samuel Huntington, President of Congress, made the first official response to the Moroccan overtures in a letter of November 28, 1780, to Franklin. Huntington wrote that Congress had received a letter from Caille, and asked Franklin to reply. Assure him, wrote Huntington, "in the name of Congress and in terms most respectful to the Emperor that we entertain a sincere disposition to cultivate the most perfect friendship with him, and are desirous to enter into a treaty of commerce with him; and that we shall embrace a favorable opportunity to announce our wishes in form."

The U.S. Government sent its first official communication to the Sultan of Morocco in December 1780. It read:

We the Congress of the 13 United States of North America, have been informed of your Majesty's favorable regard to the interests of the people we represent, which has been communicated by Monsieur Etienne d'Audibert Caille of Sale, Consul of Foreign nations unrepresented in your Majesty's states. We assure you of our earnest desire to cultivate a sincere and firm peace and

172

*friendship with your Majesty and to make it lasting to all
posterity. Should any of the subjects of our states come within
the ports of your Majesty's territories, we flatter ourselves they
will receive the benefit of your protection and benevolence. You
may assure yourself of every protection and assistance to your
subjects from the people of these states whenever and wherever
they may have it in their power. We pray your Majesty may enjoy
long life and uninterrupted prosperity.*

*No action was taken either by Congress or the Sultan for over
two years. The Americans, preoccupied with the war against
Great Britain, directed their diplomacy at securing arms, money,
military support, and recognition from France, Spain, and the
Netherlands and eventually sought peace with England.
Moreover, Sultan Sidi Muhammad and [sic] more pressing
concerns and focused on his relations with the European powers,
especially Spain and Britain over the question of Gibraltar.
From 1778 to 1782, the Moroccan leader also turned to
domestic difficulties resulting from drought and famine, and
unpopular food tax, food shortages and inflation of food prices,
trade problems, and a disgruntled military.*

*The American commissioners in Paris, John Adams, Jay, and
Franklin urged Congress in September 1783 to take some action
in negotiating a treaty with Morocco. "The Emperor of Morocco
has manifested a very friendly disposition towards us," they
wrote. "He expects and is reading to receive a Minister from us;
and as he may be succeeded by a prince differently disposed, a
treaty with him may be of importance. Our trade to the
Mediterranean will not be inconsiderable, and the friendship of
Morocco, Algiers, Tunis, and Tripoli may become very
interesting in case the Russians should succeed in their
endeavors to navigate freely into it by Constantinople."*

*Congress finally acted in the spring of 1784. On May 7,
Congress authorized its Ministers in Paris, Franklin, Jay, and
Adams, to conclude treaties of amity and commerce with Russia,*

Austria, Prussia, Denmark, Saxony, Hamburg, great Britain, Spain, Portugal, Genoa, Tuscany, Rome, Naples, Venice, Sardinia, and the Ottoman Porte as well as the Barbary States of Morocco, Algiers, Tunis, and Tripoli. The treaties with the Barbary States were to be in force for 10 years or longer. The commissioners were instructed to inform the Sultan of Morocco of the "great satisfaction which Congress feels from the amicable disposition he has shown towards these states." They were asked to state that "the occupations of the war and distance of our situation have prevented our meeting his friendship so early as we wished." A few days later, commissions were given to the three men to negotiate the treaties.

Continued delays by American officials exasperated the sultan and prompted him to take more drastic action to gain their attention. On October 11, 1784, the Moroccans captured the American merchant ship, Betsey. After the ship and crew were taken to Tangier, he announced that he would release the men, ship, and cargo once a treaty with the United States was concluded. Accordingly, preparation for negotiations with Morocco began in 1785. On March 1 Congress authorized the commissioners to delegate to some suitable agent the authority to negotiate treaties with the Barbary States. The agent was required to follow the commissioners' instructions and to submit the negotiated treaty to them for approval. Congress also empowered the commissioners to spend a maximum of 80,000 dollars to conclude treaties with these states. Franklin left Paris on July 12, 1785, to return to the United States, 3 days after the Sultan released the Betsey and its crew. Thomas Jefferson became Minister to France and thereafter negotiations were conducted by Adams in London and Jefferson in Paris. On October 11, 1785, the commissioners appointed Thomas Barclay, American Consul in Paris, to negotiate a treaty with Morocco on the basis of a draft treaty drawn up by the commissioners. That same day the commissioners appointed Thomas Lamb as special agent to negotiate a treaty with Algiers. Barclay was given a maximum of 20,000 dollars for the treaty

174

and instructed to gather information concerning the commerce, ports, naval and land forces, languages, religion, and government as well as evidence of Europeans attempting to obstruct American negotiations with the Barbary States.

Barclay left Paris on January 15, 1786, and after several stops, including 2 1/2 months in Madrid, arrived in Marrakech on June 19. While the French offered some moral support to the United States in their negotiations with Morocco, it was the Spanish government that furnished substantial backing in the form of letters from the Spanish King and Prime Minister to the Sultan of Morocco. After a cordial welcome, Barclay conducted the treaty negotiations in two audiences with Sidi Muhammad and Tahir Fannish, a leading Moroccan diplomat from a Morisco family in Sale who headed the negotiations. The earlier proposals drawn up by the American commissioners in Paris became the basis for the treaty. While the Emperor opposed several articles, the final form contained in substance all that the Americans requested. When asked about tribute, Barclay stated that he "had to offer to His Majesty the friendship of the United States and to receive his in return, to form a treaty with him on liberal and equal terms. But if any engagements for future presents or tributes were necessary, I must return without any treaty." The Moroccan leader accepted Barclay's declaration that the United States would offer friendship but no tribute for the treaty, and the question of presents or tribute was not raised again. Barclay accepted no favor except the ruler's promise to send letters to Constantinople, Tunisia, Tripoli, and Algiers recommending they conclude treaties with the United States.

Barclay and the Moroccans quickly reached agreement on the Treaty of Friendship and Amity. Also called the Treaty of Marrakech, it was sealed by the Emperor on June 23 and delivered to Barclay to sign on June 28. In addition, a separate ship seals agreement, providing for the identification at sea of American and Moroccan vessels, was signed at Marrakech on July 6, 1786. Binding for 50 years, the Treaty was signed by

*Thomas Jefferson at Paris on January 1, 1787, and John Adams
at London on January 25, 1787, and was ratified by Congress on
July 18, 1787. The negotiation of this treaty marked the
beginning of diplomatic relations between the two countries and
it was the first treaty between any Arab, Muslim, or African State
and the United States.*

*Congress found the treaty with Morocco highly satisfactory and
passed a note of thanks to Barclay and to Spain for help in the
negotiations. Barclay had reported fully on the amicable
negotiations and written that the king of Morocco had "acted in
a manner most gracious and condescending, and I really believe
the Americans possess as much of his respect and regard as does
any Christian nation whatsoever." Barclay portrayed the King as
"a just man, according to this idea of justice, of great personal
courage, liberal to a degree, a lover of his people, stern" and
"rigid in distributing justice." The Sultan sent a friendly letter to
the President of Congress with the treaty and included another
from the Moorish minister, Sidi Fennish, which was highly
complimentary of Barclay.*

*The United States established a consulate in Morocco in 1797.
President Washington had requested funds for this post in a
message to Congress on March 2, 1795, and James Simpson, the
U.S. Consul at Gibraltar who was appointed to this post, took up
residence in Tangier 2 years later. Sultan Sidi Muhammad's
successor, Sultan Moulay Soliman, had recommended to
Simpson the establishment of a consulate because he believed it
would provide greater protection for American vessels. In 1821,
the Moroccan leader gave the United States one of the most
beautiful buildings in Tangier for its consular representative.
This building served as the seat of the principal U.S.
representative to Morocco until 1956 and is the oldest piece of
property owned by the United States abroad.*

*U. S.-Moroccan relations from 1777 to 1787 reflected the
international and economic concerns of these two states in the*

late 18th century. The American leaders and the Sultan signed the 1786 treaty, largely for economic reasons, but also realized that a peaceful relationship would aid them in their relations with other powers. The persistent friendliness of Sultan Sidi Muhammad to the young republic, in spite of the fact that his overtures were initially ignored, was the most important factor in the establishment of this relationship.

The Moroccan acknowledgement of American independence seemed to be mainly a by-product of the Sultan's efforts to establish "state-controlled maritime trade" with countries with which Morocco had no treaties. However, this acknowledgement was done unilaterally on the part of Morocco, and initially there was no successful formal notification to, or formal acknowledgement by, the United States.

However, "official recognition" is what seems to be implied by people who make the claim that Morocco was the first country to recognize the United States. If the criterion for officially recognizing another country is simply to include that country's name in a document, as done by Morocco, then the honors of being the first to so recognize the United States would surely belong to Great Britain; there is no doubt that starting soon after July 4, 1776, the United States was mentioned in varying ways in many British documents! But the reality is that official recognition of a country requires more than a unilateral mention of its name in a document.

Official recognition requires a "dialogue" between the governments of independent countries. As Adam Watson, a retired British diplomat, wrote

> *States which are aware that their domestic policies are affected by 'everything that happens' outside, are not content merely to observe one another at a distance. They feel the need to enter into a dialogue with one another. This dialogue between independent states - the machinery by which their governments conduct it, and the networks of promises, contracts, institutions and codes of conduct which develop out of it - is the substance of diplomacy...diplomacy is a response to the recognition by*

several decision-making beings that the performance of each one is a matter of permanent consequence to some or all the others.[270]

The above history shows that "dialogue" between the United States and Morocco during the time period of 1776-1785 was, at best, intermittent.

But there was such a dialogue with France. Shortly after July 4, 1776, the Continental Congress began working toward achieving formal recognition from France, with the ultimate goal of forming an alliance against Great Britain. By the end of 1776 Congress had sent three Americans, Silas Deane, Arthur Lee, and Benjamin Franklin to France to work on establishing that alliance. By 1777 the French were secretly supplying the Americans with funds and weapons.

A pivotal point in American-French relations came when a British army under the leadership of General Burgoyne was defeated by the Americans at the Battle of Saratoga, and Burgoyne surrendered on October 16, 1777; the news of this defeat reached France on December 3, 1777.[271] With the defeat of the British at Saratoga, the French king decided on an official alliance with the United States.[272]

Formal negotiations began and resulted in the Treaty of Alliance, and the Treaty of Amity and Commerce with France on February 6, 1778, over two months before any United States official knew anything about a unilateral declaration by the Moroccan sultan that happened to include the name of the United States among the names of other countries. There was no treaty signed with Morocco until 1786, over eight years after these two treaties with France.

---

[270]   Adam Watson, *Diplomacy* (New York: McGraw-Hill, 1983), pp. 14-15.

[271]   John M. Blum et al., *The National Experience, A History of the United States*, 2nd ed. (New York: Harcourt, Brace and World, Inc., 1968), p. 114.

[272]   Sir Winston Churchill, *The Great Republic, A History of America*, ed. Winston S. Churchill (New York: Random House, Modern Library Paperback Edition, 2001), p. 77.

And if one wants to avoid the history, it can simply be pointed out that even according to the Office of the Historian, United States Department of State, France was the first country to recognize the United States.[273]

To make it a little easier to address this topic with others, here is a brief summary of America's early diplomatic relations:

1776

The Continental Congress sends three Americans to France to seek recognition and alliance.

1777

France secretly supplying funds and weapons to the United States.

December 3rd – News of the British defeat at Saratoga reaches France; the French King subsequently decides on a formal alliance with the United States.

December 20th – Unbeknownst to American officials, the Sultan of Morocco issues a declaration allowing access to Moroccan ports by ships from countries with which Morocco has no treaties; the United States is on the list.

1778

February 6th – Treaty of Alliance, and Treaty of Amity and Commerce between the United States and France – France officially recognizes the United States.

---

[273]   http://history.state.gov/about/faq/first-to-recognize-US; accessed May 12, 2014.

179

February 20th - Unbeknownst to American officials, the Sultan of Morocco issues a second, nearly identical declaration about access to Moroccan ports by certain countries that have no treaty with Morocco; the United States is on the list.

March – The United States establishes a consulate in Bordeaux, France.

April 14th – Etienne d'Audibert Caille was a French merchant appointed by the Sultan to serve as Consul for all the nations unrepresented in Morocco; Caille writes on behalf of the Sultan to Benjamin Franklin <u>offering to negotiate a treaty</u> between Morocco and the United States.

Late April / Early May - Benjamin Franklin receives the letter from Caille, but ignores it. Franklin later explains that he had ignored this and a subsequent letter because the French had advised him that Caille was reputed to be untrustworthy. No other American representative was aware of the correspondence.

1780

December – The United States Government sends its first official communication to the Sultan of Morocco. But no action was taken by either Congress or the Sultan for over two years.

1782

April 19th – The Republic of the Netherlands officially recognizes the United States.

1783

Treaty of Paris – Peace Treaty with Great Britain.

Spain officially recognizes the United States.

1784

October 11th - Continued delays by American officials exasperate the Sultan and prompt him to take more drastic action to gain their attention. The Moroccans capture the American merchant ship, *Betsey*. The Sultan announces that he will release the men, ship, and cargo once a treaty with the United States is concluded.

1785

Negotiations with Morocco begin.

July 9th – the Sultan releases the *Betsey* and her crew.

September - Treaty of Amity and Commerce between the United States and the King of Prussia.

1786

June – The Treaty of Friendship and Amity between the United States and Morocco was signed in Morocco.

1787

July 18th – The United States Congress ratifies the Treaty of Friendship and Amity between the United States and Morocco.

1797

The United States establishes a consulate in Tangier, Morocco.

Bibliography
(Arranged by title)

Muhammad ibn 'Abdul Wahhab At-Tamimi, *Abridged Biography of Prophet Muhammad*, ed. 'Abdur-Rahman bin Nasir Al-Barrak, 'Abdul 'Azeez bin 'Abdullah Ar-Rajihi, and Muhammad Al-'Ali Al-Barrak (Riyadh, Kingdom of Saudi Arabia: Darussalam, 2003)

Malik ibn Anas ibn Malik ibn Abi 'Amir al-Asbahi, *Al-Muwatta of Imam Malik ibn Anas: The First Formulation of Islamic Law*, trans. Aisha Abdurrahman Bewley (Inverness, Scotland: Madinah Press, 2004)

Abu'l-Hasan 'Ali ibn Ahmad ibn Muhammad ibn 'Ali al-Wahidi, *Al-Wahidi's Asbab al-Nuzul*, trans. Mokrane Guezzou (Louisville, KY: Fons Vitae, 2008)

"An Interview with the Mother of a Suicide Bomber," *Islam Review*, June 5, 2002

Mahmoud Ismail Saleh, *Dictionary of Islamic Words & Expressions*, 3rd ed. (Riyadh, Kingdom of Saudi Arabia: Darussalam, 2011)

Adam Watson, *Diplomacy* (New York: McGraw-Hill, 1983)

Essay Regarding the Basic Rule of the Blood, Wealth and Honour of the Disbelievers, At-Tibyan Publications, August 22, 2004

Fatawa Islamiyah, Islamic Verdicts, Vol. 7, collected by Muhammad bin 'Abdul-'Aziz al-Musnad, (Riyadh, Kingdom of Saudi Arabia: Darussalam, 2002)

Fatwa-Online.com

Gaidi Mtaani, Issue 4, November 2013

Joel Greenberg, "Gaza explosion kills 6 Hamas militants," *Chicago Tribune*, February 17, 2003

"Hardline Kenya cleric, the face of homegrown radical Islam," *Africatime.com*, March 11, 2014

'Imaduddeen Isma'eel ibn Katheer Al-Qurashi, *In Defence of the True Faith: Battles, Expeditions, Peace Treaties and their Consequences in the life of Prophet Muhammad*, trans. Research Department of Darussalam (Riyadh, Kingdom of Saudi Arabia: Darussalam, 2010)

Abu 'Eisa Mohammad ibn 'Eisa at-Tirmidhi, *Jami' At-Tirmidhi*, trans. Abu Khaliyl, 6 Volumes (Riyadh, Kingdom of Saudi Arabia: Darussalam, 2007)

Abu 'Abd Allah Muhammad ibn Sa'd ibn Mani' al-Zuhri al-Basri, *Kitab al-Tabaqat al-Kabir*, Vol. 2, trans. S. Moinul Haq (New Delhi, India: Kitab Bhavan, 2009)

William Yardley, "Mariam Farhat, Known as 'Mother of Martyrs,' Dies at 64," *The New York Times*, March 20, 2013

Abu Bakr Jabir Al-Jaza'iry, *Minhaj Al-Muslim*, Vol. 2, (Riyadh, Kingdom of Saudi Arabia: Darussalam, 2001)

Elior Levy, "'Mother of martyrs' dies,'" *Ynetnews.com*, March 17, 2013

Ahmad bin Muhammad bin Hanbal ash-Shaibani, *Musnad Imam Ahmad Bin Hanbal*, Vols. 1 and 2, trans. Nasiruddin Al-Khattab, ed. Huda Al-Khattab (Riyadh, Kingdom of Saudi Arabia: Darussalam, 2012)

Ahmad ibn Naqib al-Misri, *Reliance of the Traveller (Umdat al-Salik), A Classic Manual of Islamic Sacred Law*, edited and translated by Nuh Ha Mim Keller (Revised Edition 1994; rpt. Beltsville, Maryland: Amana Publications, 2008)

Muhammad bin Ismail bin Al-Mughirah Al-Bukhari, *Sahih Al-Bukhari*, trans. Muhammad Muhsin Khan, 9 Volumes (Riyadh, Kingdom of Saudi Arabia: Darussalam, 1997)

Abu'l Hussain 'Asakir-ud-Din Muslim bin Hajjaj al-Qushayri al-Naisaburi, *Sahih Muslim*, trans. Abdul Hamid Siddiqi, 8 Volumes (New Delhi: Adam Publishers and Distributors, 2008)

"Suicide Bombers' Mother Elected to Palestinian Parliament," *ABC News*, January 26, 2006

Abu Dawud Sulaiman bin Al-Ash'ath bin Ishaq, *Sunan Abu Dawud*, trans. Yaser Qadhi, 5 Volumes (Riyadh, Kingdom of Saudi Arabia: Darussalam, 2008)

Abu 'Abdur-Rahman Ahmad bin Shu'aib bin 'Ali bin Sinan bin Bahr An-Nasa'i, *Sunan An-Nasa'i*, trans. Nasiruddin al-Khattab, 6 Volumes (Riyadh, Kingdom of Saudi Arabia: Darussalam, 2007)

Muhammad bin Yazeed ibn Majah Al-Qazwini, *Sunan Ibn Majah*, trans. Nasiruddin al-Khattab, 5 Volumes (Riyadh, Kingdom of Saudi Arabia: Darussalam, 2007)

Salahuddin Yusuf, *Tafsir Ahsanul-Bayan*, trans. Mohammad Kamal Myshkat, 4 Volumes (Riyadh, Kingdom of Saudi Arabia: Darussalam, 2010)

Jalalu'd-Din Al-Mahalli and Jalalu'd-Din As-Suyuti, *Tafsir Al-Jalalayn*, trans. Aisha Bewley (London: Dar Al Taqwa Ltd., 2007)

Abu 'Abdullah Muhammad ibn Ahmad al-Ansari al-Qurtubi, *Tafsir Al-Qurtubi: Classical Commentary of the Holy Qur'an*, Vol. 1, trans. Aisha Bewley (London: Dar Al Taqwa Ltd., 2003)

Tafsir Ibn 'Abbas, trans. Mokrane Guezzou (Louisville, KY: Fons Vitae, 2008)

Abu Al-Fida' 'Imad Ad-Din Isma'il bin 'Umar bin Kathir Al-Qurashi Al-Busrawi, *Tafsir Ibn Kathir* (Abridged), trans. Jalal Abualrub, et al., 10 Volumes (Riyadh, Kingdom of Saudi Arabia: Darussalam, 2000)

The Al Qaeda Reader, trans. and ed. Raymond Ibrahim, (New York: Broadway Books, 2007)

Abi Zakaryya al-Dimashqi al-Dumyati "ibn-Nuhaas," *The Book of Jihad (Abridged)*, trans. Noor Yamani, revised by Abu Rauda, (no publisher information, 2005)

Sheikh 'Abdullah bin Muhammad bin Humaid, "The Call to Jihad (Fighting For Allah's Cause) in the Qur'an," *The Noble Qur'an*, trans. Muhammad Muhsin Khan and Muhammad Taqi-ud-Din Al-Hilali (Riyadh, Kingdom of Saudi Arabia: Maktaba Dar-us-Salam, 1994)

The Clarification Regarding Intentionally Targetting Women and Children, At-Tibyan Publications, October 31, 2004

Sir Winston Churchill, *The Great Republic, A History of America*, ed. Winston S. Churchill (New York: Random House, Modern Library Paperback Edition, 2001)

Abu Ja'far Muhammad b. Jarir al-Tabari, *The History of al-Tabari: The Conquest of Arabia*, Vol. X, trans. and annotated Fred M. Donner (Albany, New York: State University of New York Press, 1993)

Abu Ja'far Muhammad b. Jarir al-Tabari, *The History of al-Tabari: The Foundation of the Community*, Vol. VII, trans. M. V. McDonald and annotated W. Montgomery Watt (Albany, New York: State University of New York Press, 1987)

Abu Ja'far Muhammad b. Jarir al-Tabari, *The History of al-Tabari: The Last Years of the Prophet*, Vol. IX, trans. and annotated Ismail K. Poonawala (Albany, New York: State University of New York Press, 1990)

Abu Ja'far Muhammad b. Jarir al-Tabari, *The History of al-Tabari: The Victory of Islam*, Vol. VIII, trans. and annotated Michael Fishbein (Albany, New York: State University of New York Press, 1997)

Abu Hanifah Nu'man ibn Thabit ibn Nu'man ibn al-Marzuban ibn Zuta ibn Mah, *The Kitab al-Athar of Imam Abu Hanifah: The Narration of Imam Muhammad Ibn Al-Hasan Ash-Shaybani*, trans. 'Abdassamad Clarke (London: Turath Publishing, 2007)

Muhammad b. 'Umar al-Waqidi, *The Life of Muhammad: Al-Waqidi's Kitab al-Maghazi*, trans. Rizwi Faizer, Amal Ismail, and AbdulKader Tayob, ed. Rizwi Faizer, (London and New York: Routledge, 2013)

Muhammad ibn Ishaq, *The Life of Muhammad (Sirat Rasul Allah)*, trans. Alfred Guillaume (Karachi: Oxford University Press, 2007)

Imam Muwaffaq ad-Din Abdu'llah ibn Ahmad ibn Qudama al-Maqdisi, *The Mainstay Concerning Jurisprudence (Al-Umda fi 'l-Fiqh)*, trans. Muhtar Holland (Ft. Lauderdale, FL: Al-Baz Publishing, Inc., 2009)

Zareer Masani, "The Making of the Mahatma," *Standpoint*, October 2013

Shlomi Eldar, "'The Mother of Martyrs' Leaves Bloody Legacy," *Al Monitor*, March 19, 2013

John M. Blum et al., *The National Experience, A History of the United States*, 2nd ed. (New York: Harcourt, Brace and World, Inc., 1968)

The Noble Qur'an, trans. Muhammad Muhsin Khan and Muhammad Taqi-ud-Din Al-Hilali (Riyadh, Kingdom of Saudi Arabia: Darussalam, 2003)

The Noble Qur'an, trans. Muhammad Muhsin Khan and Muhammad Taqi-ud-Din Al-Hilali (Riyadh, Kingdom of Saudi Arabia: Darussalam, 2007)

Ahmad ibn Yahya ibn Jabir Al-Baladhuri, *The Origins of the Islamic State, Being a Translation from the Arabic, Accompanied with Annotations, Geographic and Historic Notes of the Kitab Fituh Al-Buldan of Al-Imam Abu-L Abbas Ahmad Ibn-Jabir Al-Baladhuri*, trans. Philip Khuri Hitti (1916; rpt. Lexington, Kentucky: Ulan Press, 2014)

Shaykh ul-Islaam Taqi ud-Deen Ahmad ibn Taymiyyah, *The Religious and Moral Doctrine of Jihaad* (Birmingham, England: Maktabah Al Ansaar Publications, 2001)

Safiur-Rahman Al-Mubarakpuri, *The Sealed Nectar* (Riyadh, Kingdom of Saudi Arabia: Darussalam, 2008)

Transcript: Speech of HSM Leader, Shaykh Mukhtar Abu Zubayr, regarding the #Westgate Operation, September 26, 2013

Majid Khadduri, *War and Peace in the Law of Islam* (Clark, NJ: The Lawbook Exchange Ltd., 2006)

'Imaduddeen Isma'eel ibn Katheer Al-Qurashi, *Winning the Hearts and Souls: Expeditions and Delegations in the Lifetime of Prophet Muhammad*, trans. Research Department of Darussalam (Riyadh, Kingdom of Saudi Arabia: Darussalam, 2010)

Muhammad bin Ahmad as-Salim ('Isa al-'Awshin), *39 Ways to Serve and Participate in Jihad*, At-Tibyan Publications, July 19, 2003

Made in the USA
Columbia, SC
09 January 2020